Building Everyday LEADERSHIP in All Kids

AN ELEMENTARY CURRICULUM
TO PROMOTE ATTITUDES AND ACTIONS
FOR RESPECT AND SUCCESS

MARIAM G. MACGREGOR, M.S.

free spirit
PUBLISHING®

Library of Congress Cataloging-in-Publication Data
MacGregor, Mariam G.
  Building everyday leadership in all kids : an elementary curriculum to promote attitudes and actions for respect and success / Mariam G. MacGregor, M.S.
     pages cm
  Includes index.
  ISBN-13: 978-1-57542-432-3
  ISBN-10: 1-57542-432-0
1. Leadership—Study and teaching (Elementary) 2. Leadership—Study and teaching (Elementary)—
Activity programs. 3. Leadership in children. I. Title.
  HM1261.M317 2013
  649'.1—dc23
                                                                2012046484

ISBN: 978-1-57542-432-3

Free Spirit Publishing does not have control over or assume responsibility for author or third-party websites and their content. At the time of this book's publication, all facts and figures cited within are the most current available. All telephone numbers, addresses, and website URLs are accurate and active as of April 2017. If you find an error or believe that a resource listed here is not as described, please contact Free Spirit Publishing. Parents, teachers, and other adults: We strongly urge you to monitor children's use of the Internet.

Some of the activities in this book are adapted from *Building Everyday Leadership in All Teens* and *Teambuilding with Teens* by Mariam G. MacGregor, M.S. Used with permission.

Edited by Eric Braun
Cover and interior design by Tasha Kenyon
Cover photo © istockphoto.com/kali9

10 9 8 7 6 5 4 3
Printed in the United States of America

Free Spirit Publishing Inc.
6325 Sandburg Road, Suite 100
Minneapolis, MN 55427-3674
(612) 338-2068
help4kids@freespirit.com
www.freespirit.com

To kids everywhere who take the initiative as
everyday leaders, in their lives and the lives of others:
Make a difference.

To my own everyday leaders—Hayes, Colt, and Lily Lake:
Do good work.

To my husband, Michael, and my editor, Eric Braun:
Thank you.

CONTENTS

*Activities contain modifications for students transitioning to middle school

LIST OF REPRODUCIBLE FORMS

You may download these forms at www.freespirit.com/BELKids-forms. Use the password potential4.

Guiding Children to Take the Lead

Perhaps you're a veteran educator, skilled and comfortable with integrating leadership education into the school day. Or maybe this is the first time you've taught a session on leadership. Maybe you've been asked to design a new program for young leaders, a daunting but rewarding task. Regardless of your background or why you're holding this book, you're in an exciting position: You're about to inspire young leaders. With your guidance, the kids in your group can gain a greater understanding of who they are and how to translate that into becoming a leader.

You might be thinking: *Elementary school is too young for leadership!* If you've been around kids enough, you know they recognize leaders in their midst from an early age. This recognition is based simply on perceived "specialness"—it's the boy who plays the best on the soccer field; it's the girl who knows all the answers when the teacher asks; it's the boy who's welcoming and nice to everyone; it's the girl who makes the entire class laugh with her jokes. But kids also see and hear about public leaders embroiled in scandals, or they hear gossip about popular "role models" like celebrities and pro athletes receiving attention for engaging in outlandish, risky, or inappropriate behaviors. They can even receive mixed messages about what it means to be a leader from people in their everyday lives: teachers, parents, coaches, youth pastors, club leaders, and peers.

This is why conducting meaningful activities and discussions on leadership behaviors,

leadership attitudes, and the difference between positive and negative leadership qualities is important. Leadership goes deeper than an individual's personality or a snapshot in the news. It's a complex mix of character traits, behaviors, skills, and competencies. Strong leaders emerge at all stages of life, and even kindergartners can benefit from identifying their own leadership strengths and weaknesses. The earlier kids learn about their leadership strengths, the sooner they can make firsthand positive differences. For example, they learn how to resolve conflict more efficiently through age-appropriate negotiation rather than fighting or tattling. They also learn the value of paying attention to the quiet students in their class in addition to the extroverts. Kids who understand leadership concepts from a young age are more likely to feel empathy and be openminded about accepting differences when working together with peers.

Much of the existing material geared to leadership for elementary students focuses on character education. Although character education is one aspect of leadership development, it's not the only one—there is also the action-oriented nature of building personal and group leadership attitudes. Increasing every child's awareness of his or her own leadership potential can have a remarkable impact on self-confidence as well as on establishing positive group dynamics. And it can increase positive character traits.

1

Making Time for Leadership

The activities in this book are designed for use in a range of settings: classrooms, after-school groups, advisory groups, service learning and leadership programs, and community- or faith-based programs.

In many cases, especially for teachers, it can feel overwhelming to determine ways to incorporate leadership activities into limited instructional minutes without feeling like it's "just another thing." But it's not as hard to make time for leadership as you might think. Here's why:

- Sessions range from 10 to 45 minutes long. Some can be easily fit into short available times, such as transitions or when you have an unexpected indoor recess due to rain. Others can be planned for as part of a standard classroom period.

- The sessions are aligned with curriculum standards, including the Common Core State Standards (see pages 9–14), so rather than being "something extra," they can support academic material you're already teaching.

- If you're already teaching character education, anti-bullying units, or social/emotional curriculum, leadership lessons are a natural way to enhance these subjects.

These activities are thoroughly classroom-tested. I have facilitated the activities in this book and others like them with more than 1,500 kids and teens since 1995. Over the years, I've heard from hundreds of teachers and youth workers from around the world about the life-changing leadership being demonstrated by kids and teens with whom they've used the curriculum. Students who have successfully completed the curriculum have benefitted in many ways, including improved academics, increased participation in class and in extracurricular activities, increased empathy, and improved confidence. So time invested in leadership pays off academically as well as socially and emotionally.

Using This Book

Building Everyday Leadership in All Kids is modeled after my *Building Everyday Leadership in All Teens* curriculum. This book provides carefully crafted leadership lessons in a format that allows you to create customized, organized leadership programs that best serve the elementary-age kids you work with.

The activities in this book are divided into nine sections organized by topic.

- **"Framing Activities"** help students establish a common understanding of what leadership means in their lives and in your setting. To lay the groundwork of such an understanding, make a framing activity one of the first ones you do with your group.

- **"Icebreakers and Warm-Ups"** are activities to establish rapport and introduce leadership basics.

- The activities in **"Understanding Leadership"** help students learn what leadership means, identify leaders in their lives, and appreciate other points of view.

- **"Becoming a Leader"** has activities on being a leader and learning about leaders and followers.

- To develop group and individual communication skills, try activities from **"Communication."**

- **"Teambuilding and Working with Others"** has activities that help build understanding about teamwork and group dynamics.

- **"Problem Solving and Decision Making"** contains activities emphasizing group and individual roles in problem solving and decision making.

- To address more complex issues related to leadership roles and responsibilities, the activities in **"Understanding Power, Values, and Relationships"** are appropriate.

- Similarly, the more complex activities in **"Making a Difference"** address broader social issues related to leadership.

With respect to limited instructional minutes (and attention spans) for 6- to 12-year-olds, the maximum activity length is 45 minutes. Most sessions fall into the range of 20 to 30 minutes, including discussion. If you conduct enrichments or extensions, which are included with many activities, you'll do these outside the timeframe of the original session.

Where necessary, sessions are divided into two sections—for younger kids (grades K–2) and older kids (grades 3–6). Different topics require different levels of maturity, physical coordination, or understanding of the subject matter, and some activities require stronger skills (such as reading, writing, and communication skills) than others to accomplish. Some examples include lessons related to ethical decision making, teambuilding, communication, power, and identifying leaders in one's life.

The sessions are designed with the goal of engaging all emerging leaders, regardless of emotional and academic levels. Each session is designed to promote group interaction, build self-confidence, and allow kids to explore intrapersonal understanding, even if they don't yet fully know what these things are. The sessions also allow older kids to be challenged both inter- and intrapersonally as they learn to fully identify and fine-tune their leadership abilities.

Each session in this book opens with an activity summary and also has:

- **Time, Age, Group Size:** The anticipated time necessary to conduct the session, suggested audience age by grade, and recommended group size

- **Leadership Learning Concepts:** A list of the primary leadership concepts addressed by the session (see page 4)

- **Supporting Standards:** The academic standards supported by the session

- **Materials Needed:** What you'll need to conduct the session; a complete list of materials needed for all activities is on page 196

- **Getting Ready:** Steps to prepare for conducting the session

- **Activity:** The main part of the session, this includes step-by-step guidance to conducting the activity with your group

- **Talk About It:** Discussion questions to use with the group following the activity

Some sessions include:

- **Variations:** Ideas that modify the original activity to more effectively incorporate the activity with different audiences such as younger or older kids or to differentiate the activity with your specific group.

- **Enrichments:** Ideas that add breadth and strengthen leadership learning during the lesson. Enrichments can be used during the activity to increase challenge or to engage kids in different ways.

- **Extensions:** Ideas that extend the learning and create deeper connections for the lesson. Extensions are relevant as follow-up to the specific lesson, during another group gathering or class period, or for homework or out-of-session projects.

- Reproducible handouts that you can photocopy from the book or access as customizable PDFs at the Free Spirit Publishing website at freespirit.com/BELKids-forms (password potential4). Some handouts are meant for your use, but most are intended to be distributed to the kids you're working with. In some cases, two versions of a handout are available—one for kids in grades 3–6 and one for kids in grades K–2. The handouts intended for younger students have a notebook paper design and a larger title; handouts for older students have a simple frame and a smaller title.

Grades 3–6   Grades K–2

Read through each session completely before conducting it so you're familiar with the goals, process, and any background information. This preparation also helps you anticipate any barriers kids might encounter in understanding the material, special topics or modifications you want to consider, or ways you might want to incorporate possible variations, extensions, enrichments, or discussion emphasis specific to the needs of your group.

If you have students with physical challenges—for example, requiring crutches or a wheelchair—you may need to consider modifications to the sessions. The majority of the sessions can be conducted with few or no changes. For some activities, suggestions are provided.

Leadership Learning Concepts

Leadership Learning Concepts are the skills and competencies addressed in each activity. Some sessions may touch on several concepts, while others touch on only one or two. The list below provides a brief definition of every concept.

- **Active Listening:** Learning to actively hear and process information being verbally communicated

- **Appreciating Others:** Giving others encouragement and recognition for hard work and doing things well

- **Building Friendships:** Learning and practicing appropriate behaviors for building positive relationships with others

- **Bullies, Cliques, and Peer Pressure:** Recognizing behaviors, positive and negative, that can occur when groups of kids get together; understanding one's role and responsibilities when these behaviors are taking place

- **Communication:** Skill building related to public speaking, active listening, giving and receiving feedback, constructive criticism, nonverbal messages, etc.

- **Creative Thinking:** Discovering new ways of thinking and problem solving

- **Decision Making:** Learning how to make confident decisions as individuals and as part of a group

- **Discernment:** Determining what's important to notice and what's not; learning to pay attention to details; developing the ability to prioritize

- **Ethics:** Learning how to discern between right and wrong and how to make decisions when dealing with dilemmas and life's "gray" areas

- **Feedback:** Learning how to give and receive messages of support or ideas for improvement

- **First Impressions:** How to make a positive first impression and why it's important

- **Getting to Know Others:** Going beyond name games and introductions to uncover what makes others in the group "tick"

- **Goal Setting:** Deciding what a team or individual wants and the steps necessary to achieve those goals

- **Group Dynamics:** What happens when groups of people get together, especially if they have different ideas or may not be part of a team

- **Leadership Basics:** What it means to be a leader and general concepts related to leadership

- **Observation Skills:** Paying attention to and learning from other people and situations

- **Patience:** Learning how to deal with situations calmly and without getting upset

- **Problem Solving:** Identifying methods that work to solve problems successfully; learning more about how conflict can lead to positive results

- **Public Speaking:** Strengthening the skills necessary to comfortably present and speak in front of others

- **Qualities of Leadership:** Recognizing the characteristics commonly seen or expected in leaders

- **Resourcefulness:** Being imaginative in different situations and coming up with creative ways to overcome obstacles

- **Risk Taking:** Understanding the basics of risks leaders may need to take and the difference between appropriate everyday risks and dangerous everyday risks

- **Role Models and Mentors:** Developing skills to serve as a positive role model or mentor (someone others want to be like, follow, or learn from) as well as identifying the qualities one expects from their role models and mentors; also, understanding the difference between individuals admired for their popularity and "celebrity" status, and those who are admired because of their social influence as leaders

- **Self-Awareness:** Uncovering and sharing what one knows about oneself

- **Self-Disclosure:** Sharing more about oneself including personal values and experiences

- **Teamwork:** Building the skills necessary to promote working together, positive group dynamics, and success as a team; learning how to work productively with others

- **Tolerance and Diversity:** Learning to interact with, get along with, and seek out people with different opinions and backgrounds from oneself

- **Understanding Social Change:** Learning how to make a difference for causes and issues that are important to individuals

- **Values:** Exploring the beliefs and opinions that each person considers important and learning to respect the differences among individuals

Middle School Transition Modifications

Some sessions, marked in the contents with an asterisk and listed on page 15, are particularly relevant for students transitioning to middle school. For these activities, modifications are included that frame the sessions and discussion questions around concerns facing fifth- and sixth-grade students as they prepare to enter middle school. Examples of leadership issues related to middle school include peer pressure, decision making, handling ethical

dilemmas, finding your voice, supporting friends in difficult situations, and being your best self. These activities can be made even more powerful by having high school students serve as facilitators and discussion guides. If time permits, incorporate these activities on a regular basis (once a week or once every other week, for example) during the final semester or trimester of elementary school.

You might also consider hosting an "everything you want to know about middle school but are afraid to ask" panel toward the end of the school year, where a group of high school students presents to or interacts with fifth or sixth graders about the transition. Prep the high school students ahead of time to discuss ways to respond to your students' questions in appropriate ways. Limit the number of adults in the room to a school counselor or psychologist and a different grade or subject area teacher or two who have strong rapport with the students. Having their current fifth- or sixth-grade teachers in the room during the panel can often be counterproductive to creating an open, safe atmosphere for kids to feel comfortable disclosing their concerns and worries. Some kids feel judged or nervous that their teacher will think differently of them in the classroom based on the questions they ask the high school panel.

Setting the Tone

The activities in this book are built on student-directed learning. To be most effective, lead as a facilitator rather than an "instructor." This helps students learn the leadership lessons and concepts through their interactions with one another. Because leadership topics inspire self-reflection and disclosure, it is essential to promote a safe environment that encourages supportive attitudes for and from everyone. Here are some guidelines:

Divide Large Groups into Smaller Groups

Some activities guide you to divide the larger group into smaller teams or groups. If your large group is fairly homogenous or your goals for the activity won't be impacted by peer pressure or existing relationships, you can create smaller groups randomly at the time of the session. You might do this by passing out colored stickers representing each team, inviting kids to count off or select colored toothpicks or marbles from a bag, or using other equitable, objective methods for dividing into equally numbered groups.

More often, you'll want to select the teams ahead of time because leadership learning is enriched when kids interact with others different from themselves. How you do this will vary depending on your setting and individual group. If the group is mixed-gender, strive to have a balance of boys and girls regardless of the age of the group. If culture, background, or other factors impact the relationships among kids in the group, determine ahead of time the best ways to make the smaller teams as diverse as possible.

Kids in early elementary generally thrive when together with friends on a team. This allows the relationships they share to play a role. Of course, kids can be fickle when it comes to friendships, so you may find yourself changing the makeup of groups throughout the year. For older students, evaluate the dynamics of the larger group to determine if friends might learn more by being on different teams or if the arrangement is inconsequential. When working with students in their final year of elementary school, you can divide teams based on each of the schools they'll attend (if they're not all going to the same school).

For all groups, you'll want to balance the "talkers" with students who may be more reserved. Pay attention that talkers don't dominate the activity. Develop a personal plan for engaging shyer or hesitant students in the activity. Sometimes, this is as simple as requiring everyone in the group to give their opinion, answer a question, or take a turn in a leadership role. Other times, you will find yourself addressing overbearing students directly by gently suggesting the group hear from others, dividing them from their peer group, or putting them into "listening" roles.

Emphasize Confidentiality

Elementary-age children can be inexperienced with social cues and appropriate discussion process. When one student offers a comment or insight on the activity, other kids easily latch on to one or two words in the response and quickly shift the conversation away from the true topic at hand. Similarly, young kids often lack the ability to filter what they say and to recognize when to keep shared information to themselves—within a group, between individuals, and in other company outside their classroom. Maintain an atmosphere within the group that's respectful of diverse opinions. It's a good idea before your first session to talk about what it means when information is "confidential," and follow up periodically with reminders to honor everyone's confidentiality. Help kids practice ways to avoid using people's personal information or real names when talking about their leadership lessons, both within and outside your group.

When conducting the sessions, you may discover that some topics evoke personal admissions and highly charged situations. It's hard to predict exactly when someone may become affected by emotion or when conflict may arise within the group. But if you establish trust early on with the group and monitor any particular dynamics between members, you likely will be able to anticipate potentially difficult circumstances. If intense moments occur, help those who may disagree with one another to talk it through.

Encourage Full Engagement

Because the activities in this book are designed to be fun and appealing, they easily engage kids. Still, some kids initially may be uncomfortable taking the risks necessary to lead or participate fully in session activities. Some may not understand the broader context of the activity or not "get" the whole leadership thing. Clarify concepts in a manner that stretches the thinking of every child, while recognizing that some kids will grasp abstract connections quicker than others.

Recognize the developmental context and fickle behavior of younger children (one day they're easily engaged, the next they have a hard time focusing). Encourage kids to participate at their highest level of understanding, and pay attention if kids are having a hard time grasping the concepts you're teaching. If necessary, remind kids of all the simple ways they can practice being a leader.

Most kids thrive when genuinely encouraged to try new things, especially if they doubt their ability, are unsure of their capabilities, or get nervous about what others might think. One way to encourage a shy or reserved child is to create an opportunity to take on a speaking role in an activity but not necessarily take the lead. Overall, your sensitivity to the children's perspective is essential.

Set some basic ground rules just as you would when striving to establish an overall positive classroom culture. Remind kids that revealing personal information isn't always necessary to demonstrate they've learned something from an activity. If kids start to act overly silly or lose focus, stop an activity and remind them of its purpose.

As kids develop self-confidence and comfort in practicing and developing leadership skills, encourage their involvement and create leadership opportunities within the larger group. Even if some kids at first choose to participate minimally, it probably won't be long before they feel they are missing out by not joining in.

Get the Most Out of Role Playing

Some of these activities utilize role playing. Role playing provides participants a fun opportunity to experience different perspectives in small or large groups. Kids assume the roles of certain characters to act out in various scenarios. Review the roles with participants before starting an activity and remind them to stay in character throughout the role play. Tell participants that they never have to reveal personal information in role playing.

When kids practice different roles, the learning takes on a real-life aspect. This makes it easier to apply particular strategies when actual situations arise. Role playing in the sessions is scripted in order to achieve an expected outcome, but participants will

still connect personally to the topic. Role playing is most meaningful when participants and observers also discuss their reactions to the role play afterward and its application to real life.

Practice Skills

Because kids in grades K–6 are at different levels of maturity and cognitive development, opportunities you create for further discussion and practicing skills will vary by age and setting. A sixth-grade student preparing to enter middle school generally has greater capacity to apply his or her leadership learning to broader life situations, whereas a kindergarten or first-grade child is more apt to learn by applying the lesson to immediate situations.

Some session activities depend upon having kids take on a leadership role. You can increase leadership practice for all kids, especially as they move beyond second grade, by assigning different kids to lead the "Talk About It" discussion. Depending on the nature of the kids with whom you work, you may find that asking them prior to the session increases confidence to take this role, or you may have kids who eagerly jump at any chance to lead either an activity or a discussion.

At other times, you may want to randomly pick a name (or names) from a box or hat. Meet with the chosen student(s) ahead of time to prepare him or her to lead the activity from start to finish. Create strategies to encourage shy or hesitant kids to give it a try and promote the activity as an opportunity rather than a requirement. Some of the Extensions included with different activities provide excellent ways for kids to bump up their leadership skills practice.

Aside from leading the activity or the discussion, you can also find school- and community-wide opportunities for kids to take on leadership roles. These can include participating in student council, serving as book buddies with younger students, running Field Day events, helping or mentoring other kids in the classroom, and promoting and coordinating service projects and fundraising activities for the school. (Yes, elementary kids can and should be expected to be more in charge of these activities instead of having only parents and PTO associations run them!) Set a high bar and kids will achieve—and exceed—your expectations.

Decide which approach works best for your kids and your setting, involving different kids throughout the sessions so everyone gets a chance to practice skills. To engage as many students as possible, you may need to divide the class into smaller groups that will simultaneously participate in an activity. If your group size is much smaller, decrease the number of students per group when working in small groups or eliminate observers during role playing.

Before you begin teaching kids more about leadership, take time to think through your own definitions, expectations, biases, and personal behaviors related to leadership, especially if you doubt the ability of young kids to grasp such an immense subject. No matter how organized and well-designed your lesson plan is, if you struggle with integrating leadership as a life-long behavior, your sessions will fall flat.

Aligning with Standards

The leadership activities in this book are aligned with Common Core State Standards in the subjects of English Language Arts (ELA) and Mathematics; Colorado state standards in Social Studies & Civics and Health and Physical Education (standards in your state are likely similar); and the National Youth Leadership Council Service-Learning Standards for Quality Practice. Requirements to align your curriculum with standards in these areas do not mean

less time for other subjects like leadership because there are many ways to integrate leadership education into your lessons. While I have aligned the lessons with these specific standards, you can easily align them with your state's standards whether it has adopted the Common Core or not.

In fact, integrating leadership in the classroom supports and enriches core subject matter while positively impacting group dynamics. For example, writing prompts in language arts can involve leadership topics; a civics lesson in social studies can include a discussion on how decisions are made in the broader community setting. Students not only address specific academic content, they also learn how to use their individual "leadership attitudes" to interact and communicate successfully with peers.

The following tables show specific correlations between the lessons in this book and standards. Because many of the leadership lessons address a wide range of topics, you may want to explore the Common Core State Standards or your state standards more deeply to determine how the lessons align with additional standards. You can find the full standards at the following links:

- Common Core State Standards Initiative Home Page: www.corestandards.org

- National Youth Leadership Council Standards: www.nylc.org/standards

- State of California Content Standards: www.cde.ca.gov/be/st/ss

- State of Colorado Department of Education: www.cde.state.co.us

English Language Arts: Common Core State Standards (ELA)

These tables align lessons with the broad "Anchor Standards" for the Common Core in ELA, which cover grades K–5. To read more about these standards, and to get grade-specific standards for your grade level, visit the Common Core website at www.corestandards.org.

Anchor Standards for Gr. K–5 Speaking and Listening (ELA—Speaking and Listening)*
The following activities from this book can be used to reinforce ELA—Speaking and Listening standards: Defining Leadership, All About Us Bingo, Concentration, Leadership Talk Show, Martian Names, Future News Makers, Leaders in My Life, Connections, What's in a Name?, Everyday Dilemmas, Count Off, The Accidental Witness, Leadership Improv, Puzzle, Snowflake, Group Juggling, Spaghetti Train Obstacle Course, Pipeline, Would You Rather?, Humpty Dumpty, Time Capsule Transfer, Choose a Flag, Smirk, More Like Me, Inside Out, What's It Worth?, Choosing Sides, Change the World, It Could Be Worse
Comprehension and Collaboration
Prepare for and participate effectively in a range of conversations and collaborations with diverse partners, building on others' ideas and expressing their own clearly and persuasively.
Integrate and evaluate information presented in diverse media and formats, including visually, quantitatively, and orally.
Evaluate a speaker's point of view, reasoning, and use of evidence and rhetoric.
Presentation of Knowledge and Ideas
Present information, findings, and supporting evidence such that listeners can follow the line of reasoning and the organization, development, and style are appropriate to task, purpose, and audience.
Make strategic use of digital media and visual displays of data to express information and enhance understanding of presentations.
Adapt speech to a variety of contexts and communicative tasks, demonstrating command of formal English when indicated or appropriate.

Anchor Standards for Gr. K–5 Writing (ELA—Writing)*
The following activities from this book can be used to reinforce ELA—Writing standards: Defining Leadership, Leadership Acrostic, Handprints, Future News Makers, Egg Hunt, Word List Feedback, Back/Feedback, Change the World
Text Types and Purposes
Write arguments to support claims in an analysis of substantive topics or texts, using valid reasoning and relevant and sufficient evidence.
Write informative/explanatory texts to examine and convey complex ideas and information clearly and accurately through the effective selection, organization, and analysis of content.
Write narratives to develop real or imagined experiences or events using effective technique, well-chosen details, and well-structured event sequences.

Production and Distribution of Writing
Produce clear and coherent writing in which the development, organization, and style are appropriate to task, purpose, and audience.
Develop and strengthen writing as needed by planning, revising, editing, rewriting, or trying a new approach.
Use technology, including the Internet, to produce and publish writing and to interact and collaborate with others.
Research to Build and Present Knowledge
Conduct short as well as more sustained research projects based on focused questions, demonstrating understanding of the subject under investigation.
Gather relevant information from multiple print and digital sources, assess the credibility and accuracy of each source, and integrate the information while avoiding plagiarism.
Draw evidence from literary or informational texts to support analysis, reflection, and research.
Range of Writing
Write routinely over extended time frames (time for research, reflection, and revision) and shorter time frames (a single sitting or a day or two) for a range of tasks, purposes, and audiences.

Anchor Standards for Gr. K–5 Language (ELA—Language)*

The following activities from this book can be used to reinforce ELA—Language standards: Defining Leadership, Leadership Acrostic, Martian Names, Leaders in My Life, Connections, Word List Feedback, Leadership Improv, Back/Feedback, More Like Me, Change the World
Conventions of Standard English
Demonstrate command of the conventions of standard English grammar and usage when writing or speaking.
Knowledge of Language
Apply knowledge of language to understand how language functions in different contexts, to make effective choices for meaning or style, and to comprehend more fully when reading or listening.
Vocabulary Acquisition and Use
Determine or clarify the meaning of unknown and multiple-meaning words and phrases by using context clues, analyzing meaningful word parts, and consulting general and specialized reference materials, as appropriate.
Demonstrate understanding of word relationships and nuances in word meanings.
Acquire and use accurately a range of general academic and domain-specific words and phrases sufficient for reading, writing, speaking, and listening at the college and career readiness level; demonstrate independence in gathering vocabulary knowledge when encountering an unknown term important to comprehension or expression.

Mathematics: Common Core State Standards

The Common Core does not identify Anchor Standards for Mathematics. Specific grade level standards for math are available on the Common Core State Standards website, but because of their depth and detail, it would be cumbersome to list them all in this book. Leadership lessons that contribute to mathematical proficiency usually relate to ideas such as problem solving, reasoning and proof, communication, and connections. Visiting www.corestandards.org/Math/Practice will take you to the individual grade level standards for math where you can identify ways to emphasize the math standard for your classroom and age level.

Standards for Grades K–6 Mathematics
The following activities from this book can be used to reinforce Mathematics standards: Blanket Ping Pong, Brick Houses, Count Off, House of Cards, Puzzle, Birthday Line Up, Group Juggling, Pipeline, Humpty Dumpty, Magic Carpet, What's It Worth?, Zapping Maze

Social Studies Standards

The Common Core does not contain social studies standards, but all states have standards in this area. This table contains excerpts of standards from the state of Colorado, which may be representative of or similar to those of your state.

State Standards for Grades K–6 Social Studies*
The following activities from this book can be used to reinforce Social Studies standards: Defining Leadership, Concentration, All About Us Bingo, Famous Pairs, Leaders in My Life, Leadership Treasure Hunt, Everyday Dilemmas, Choose a Flag, Would You Rather?, Smirk, Inside Out, What's It Worth?, More Like Me, Change the World, Choosing Sides, Zapping Maze, It Could Be Worse
Civics
Analyze and debate multiple perspectives on an issue (Gr. 4 and up)
Respecting the views and rights of others as components of a democratic society (Gr. 3 and up)
People use multiple ways to resolve conflicts or differences (Gr. 2 and up)
Responsible community members advocate for their ideas (Gr. 2 and up)
Effective groups have responsible leaders and team members (Gr. 1 and up)
Participate in making decisions using democratic traditions (Gr. K and up)

*www.cde.state.co.us. Used with permission.

Health and Physical Education Standards

There are many leadership concepts that students learn through health and physical education classes and team sports. This table contains excerpts of physical education standards from the state of Colorado, which include health standards, and which may be representative of or similar to those of your state.

Standards for Grades K–6 Comprehensive Physical Education*
The following activities from this book can be used to reinforce Health and Physical Education standards: Balloon Train, Linked, Blanket Ping Pong, What I Look for in My Friends, Brick Houses, Squeeze, House of Cards, Birthday Line Up, Group Juggling, Pretzel Pass, Spaghetti Train Obstacle Course, Pipeline, Island Statues, Time Capsule Transfer
Movement Competence and Understanding
Participate in activities that require problem solving, cooperation, skill assessment, and teambuilding (Gr. 6)
Perform movements that engage the brain to facilitate learning (Gr. 3 and up)
Use feedback to improve performance (Gr. 2 and up)
Emotional and Social Wellness
Recognize diverse skill performance in others and how that diversity affects game, activity, and sport participation (Gr. 6)
Work cooperatively and productively in a group (Gr. 6 and up)
Assess and take responsibility for personal behavior and stress management (Gr. 5 and up)
Demonstrate positive social behaviors during class (Gr. 3 and up)
Demonstrate positive and helpful behavior and words toward other students (Gr. 2 and up)
Work independently and with others to complete work (Gr. 1 and up)
Follow the rules of an activity (Gr. 1 and up)
Demonstrate respect for self, others, and equipment (Gr. K and up)
Demonstrate the ability to follow directions (Gr. K and up)
Prevention and Risk Management
Apply rules, procedures, and safe practices to create a safe school environment with little or no reinforcement (Gr. 2 and up)

*www.cde.state.co.us. Used with permission.

Service-Learning Standards

Leadership education and service-learning efforts are closely related and easy to align. These standards were developed by the National Youth Leadership Council, a recognized leader in promoting service learning.

Standards for Grades K–6 Service Learning*
The following activities from this book can be used to reinforce the Service-Learning standards: Concentration, All About Us Bingo, Famous Pairs, Handprints, Future News Makers, Leaders in My Life, What I Look for in My Friends, Leadership Treasure Hunt, Egg Hunt, What's in a Name?, Everyday Dilemmas, Island Statues, Would You Rather?, Smirk, Inside Out, More Like Me, What's It Worth?, Change the World, Choosing Sides, Zapping Maze, It Could Be Worse
Meaningful Service Service learning actively engages participants in meaningful and personally relevant service activities.
Link to Curriculum Service learning is intentionally used as an instructional strategy to meet learning goals and/or content standards.
Reflection Service learning incorporates multiple challenging reflection activities that are ongoing and that prompt deep thinking and analysis about oneself and one's relationship to society.
Diversity Service learning promotes understanding of diversity and mutual respect among all participants.
Youth Voice Service learning provides youth with a strong voice in planning, implementing, and evaluating service-learning experiences with guidance from adults.
Partnerships Service-learning partnerships are collaborative, mutually beneficial, and address community needs.
Progress Monitoring Service learning engages participants in an ongoing process to assess the quality of implementation and progress toward meeting specified goals, and uses results for improvement and sustainability.
Duration and Intensity Service learning has sufficient duration and intensity to address community needs and meet specified outcomes.

*The K–12 Service-Learning Standards for Quality Practice. Copyright © 2008 National Youth Leadership Council. www.nylc.org. Used with permission.

Leadership Competencies

Although there are no recognized or agreed-upon national content standards for teaching leadership in the United States or Canada, standards are being developed and established at the state and provincial levels. When you conduct sessions from this book, regardless of context, kids will be exposed to core leadership competencies I've developed over the years, based on my professional experience as a leadership educator. These leadership competencies align with content standards for leadership, service learning, or career preparation that have been established or are being implemented in several states.

- Understand what it means to be a leader and recognize ways to be a leader in everyday situations.

- Recognize how people lead and how to be a leader and help others be leaders as well.

- Begin to explore how people use power and influence with others.

- Begin to make confident decisions, even when others may try to convince them differently.

- Gain age-appropriate understanding of what it means to be part of a diverse society, including confronting prejudice and stereotypes and including others.

- Begin to learn what it means to be responsible, follow through, speak up appropriately, and support friends to do the right thing and stand up for their beliefs.
- Learn how to work with people who are different from them.
- Learn and practice effective ways to resolve conflict and solve problems.
- Explore various leadership topics and skills such as motivation, communication, setting and achieving goals, qualities of leadership, teamwork, valuing others, and broader social issues.
- Identify appropriate role models and demonstrate effective leadership for others.
- Accept and learn from mistakes and celebrate team successes appropriately.
- Act confidently as a leader and be recognized for leadership actions that demonstrate how to make an ongoing difference, whether big or small, as an everyday leader.

Sequencing Suggestions

The sessions in this book are self-contained and can be conducted in any order you choose to best fit your particular setting, student capabilities, and the context of any other instruction you're doing. For most groups, particularly those that have little or no prior experience with leadership instruction, I recommend doing one of the Framing Activities (pages 17–23) first or second. These are designed to help form a basic understanding of what leadership is, setting the stage for more in-depth understanding when you do subsequent activities.

Here are five session sequences to consider. Each sequence consists of 10 to 12 sessions to be conducted during separate meeting times. While certain activities are best done earlier in the process (like those from the Icebreakers and Warm-Ups section), you can be flexible on the order you ultimately choose. Read through each activity completely and consider the maturity level and needs of your particular group.

These sequences are simply suggestions. Over time, as you conduct each session from the book in your own setting, you will find other sequences that are effective for your needs. A blank page is included for you to document sequences for future reference (see page 16).

Early Grades (K–2) Intro to Leadership

1. Balloon Train (page 26)
2. Defining Leadership (page 18)
3. Linked (page 28)
4. Handprints (page 65)
5. Leadership Acrostic (page 20)
6. Count Off (page 97)
7. Squeeze (page 103)
8. Birthday Line Up (page 120)
9. Humpty Dumpty (page 142)
10. Magic Carpet (page 139)
11. Smirk (page 158)
12. Change the World (page 180)

Building Self-Awareness (Learning More About Myself as a Leader)

1. Blanket Ping Pong (page 46)
2. Framing Activity (choose one, pages 18–23)
3. Famous Pairs (page 32)
4. Leaders in My Life (page 55)
5. What I Look for in My Friends (page 72)
6. Egg Hunt (page 80)
7. Snowflake (page 114)
8. Pretzel Pass (page 122)
9. Would You Rather? (page 136)
10. Inside Out (page 168)
11. Choosing Sides (page 183)

Being a Leader in Action

1. Concentration (page 30)
2. Framing Activity (choose one, pages 18–23)
3. All About Us Bingo (page 35)

Middle School Transition Activities (Grades 5–6)

(**Note:** The Middle School Transition Activities are not in any particular order; use any or all throughout the school year with your students who are transitioning to middle school.)

The Next Step

For many kids, deliberate, organized education related to leadership is new territory. The same may be true for you, too. Teaching leadership to young people not only helps kids learn more about themselves and become better team players and leaders, but it also helps *adults* improve their own leadership characteristics and become the role models kids need.

By incorporating leadership into your classroom, you enrich every child's elementary experience. You also contribute to a long-lasting confidence related to learning and practicing everyday leadership skills. In addition to building this confidence, you send well-prepared young leaders into the world to pursue the next step in their leadership journey—a journey that lasts a lifetime.

If you have any questions or would like to share stories of ways you've successfully included leadership education in your efforts with kids, I'd love to hear from you. Contact me through Free Spirit Publishing at help4kids@freespirit.com or visit my website at www.mariammacgregor.com.

Mariam G. MacGregor

My Sequence

1. _____
   _____
2. _____
   _____
3. _____
   _____
4. _____
   _____
5. _____
   _____
6. _____
   _____
7. _____
   _____
8. _____
   _____
9. _____
   _____
10. _____
    _____
11. _____
    _____
12. _____
    _____
13. _____
    _____
14. _____
    _____
15. _____
    _____

Framing ACTIVITIES

1. Defining Leadership (Grades K–6)

2. Leadership Acrostic (Grades K–6)

To create a context for leadership activities, it's important that every child in the group, regardless of age, has a definition and personal context for defining leadership (the term), the qualities he or she expects in leaders, and what leadership "looks like" to him or her. The sessions in this section help achieve that common understanding of what leadership means to kids. Right before or after facilitating a session from the Icebreakers and Warm-Ups chapter—but before teaching deeper leadership lessons—you may find it useful to conduct one of these two framing activities.

SESSION · SESSION · SESSION · SESSION

1

DEFINING
Leadership

In this session, kids create their own definitions of leadership based on the words they brainstorm in small groups. This activity is useful for introducing leadership as a higher level concept than being "nice," "popular," or "a good athlete."

Time: 30 minutes (with discussion)

Age: Grades K–6

Group Size: No limit; kids work in groups of 4–10

LEADERSHIP LEARNING CONCEPTS

- Leadership Basics
- Qualities of Leadership

SUPPORTING STANDARDS

This activity supports content standards in ELA—Speaking and Listening, ELA—Language, and Social Studies (see pages 9–14 for details).

MATERIALS NEEDED

- markers
- chart paper

Activity

There are many definitions of leadership. People have different opinions about what leaders do, and how and why we think someone is a leader. If we think only of people in positions of power, such as teachers, coaches, police officers, and politicians, the majority of individuals will be overlooked for the ways they truly act as leaders in daily interactions.

For example, here's the definition of leadership I often use with kids:

Leadership is doing the right thing, being honest, being humble, and making confident decisions, even in difficult situations where others may pressure you to act differently. Leadership also means treating others as you want to be treated. Good leaders help others along so their "team" (family/class/school) thrives and succeeds because they're prepared for the challenges in each day.

Use this definition for this activity, or one you develop on your own that is easy for kids in your group to understand. Write it on the board, display it on the interactive whiteboard, or print it on a large sheet of paper visible by everyone.

Have a group discussion about what it means to brainstorm. Ask kids to explain in their own words what brainstorming means, and remind them that in brainstorming, all ideas are accepted and written down and no one comments either positively or negatively on any of the ideas. Then divide the kids into small groups.

Explain the activity like this:

In your small groups, brainstorm words or phrases (positive and negative) that come to mind when I say the word "leadership" or "leader." Think about words that describe leaders and leadership. Can anyone give me an example?

Here are a few age-appropriate examples.

Kids in kindergarten through second grade might say a leader is someone who:

- gets along well with others
- doesn't bully
- is polite
- respects others
- follows rules
- can tell you what he or she thinks
- stays on task

Kids in third through sixth grade might say a leader is someone who:

- stands up for others
- shows respect
- is trustworthy
- is dependable
- is motivated
- works hard
- withstands peer pressure
- has clear opinions

As the groups are brainstorming, circulate around the room to review their lists and make sure all group members are engaged and staying on task. Give them about five minutes.

Take the next 10 to 15 minutes to have each group present its list of leadership characteristics to the larger group. Ask for one or two volunteers to write all of the words on chart paper or a whiteboard as each group presents its list. The recorder can use hatch marks to identify duplicates. You may want to leave the chart paper visible to keep these leadership characteristics in mind during additional sessions. (If possible, following the session, create a community list by typing all of the words onto a master list. Distribute copies of the list at the next session for kids to use for future reference.)

Talk About It

Using terms your students will understand, ask questions like the following to help explore the leadership learning:

- Was it easy to come up with words to describe leadership? Or was it hard? Why?

- Do you think any ideas on your lists are negative descriptions of leadership or leaders? What are a few examples? Why do you think these words come to mind?

- What ideas did every group list? Why do you think these terms are so common?

- When you think of the people who are leaders in your life, which of the ideas on your list describe them?

- If you want people to think of you as a leader, how do you hope they would describe you?

- What ideas from your lists are unrealistic (or unfair) to expect in a leader? (For example: perfect, flawless, always right, or other characteristics that the groups shared.)

- In general, what do you expect of leaders? Do you think it's realistic or fair to expect that? Why or why not? What do you think, feel, or do when leaders don't live up to your expectations?

SESSION · SESSION · SESSION · SESSION

2

LEADERSHIP
Acrostic

Using the acrostic approach to writing, kids strengthen language arts skills and leadership awareness at the same time. To promote group interaction, use one of the two variations, which require kids to work to accomplish the task in teams of three to five.

Time: 30 minutes (with discussion)

Age: Grades K–6

Group Size: No limit

LEADERSHIP LEARNING CONCEPTS

* Leadership Basics
* Qualities of Leadership
* Creative Thinking

SUPPORTING STANDARDS

This activity supports content standards in ELA—Writing and ELA—Language (see pages 9–14 for details).

MATERIALS NEEDED

* "Leadership Acrostic" handout for grades 3–6 (page 22) or "Leadership Letters" handout for grades K–2 (page 23)
* chart paper (for Variation 2)
* markers (for Variation 2)
* tape

Getting Ready

Make one copy of the "Leadership Acrostic" or "Leadership Letters" handout for each person.

Activity

Decide if you want kids to write their acrostic as a poem that relates to leadership and leaders or simply as a collection of words that relate to and create the word "LEADER" or "LEADERSHIP." (See the following examples of each).

If creating acrostics is a new concept, give a brief lesson on the writing approach: *An acrostic starts with a topic word that is written vertically (going down the side of a page). Each letter in that word then starts a line in a poem or a single word in a list. Whether it's a poem or list of words, each line relates to the topic word.*

You may want to provide an example using your name or other word associated with leadership. Here are two examples (poem and collection of words) using the word LEADER:

POEM	WORDS
Lifting	**L**oyal
Everyone's spirits	**E**nthusiastic
And getting a project	**A**ppreciative
Done	**D**etermined
Earns	**E**ncouraging
Respect	**R**esponsible

Once everyone understands what an acrostic is, have them create their own (if doing it individually) or create one in a small group (see Variations 1 and 2).

When completed, ask for volunteers to present their completed acrostics to the whole group.

Talk About It

Using terms your students will understand, ask questions like the following to help explore the leadership learning:

- Which letter was the easiest to start a line with?

- Were any letters harder than others to find words to fit? Explain.

- How were the acrostics alike? How were they different? Why do you think some things were alike and some different?

- Do you think it will be easier to explain what leadership means now that you've come up with words or statements that "show" what it means to you? Explain.

Variations

1. Divide the large group into smaller groups of three to five kids and make one copy of the handout for each small group. In place of having kids work on their acrostics independently, have the small groups brainstorm and work together to create a group acrostic.

2. Divide the large group into small groups of three to five kids and have each group brainstorm together to create, draw, and decorate a group acrostic poster. Provide each group with one poster-size piece of chart paper and one box or bag of markers. When every group has finished, hang up the posters on the wall.

3. Rather than having kids create acrostics with the word "LEADERSHIP," have them use their own names and make a poem that shows how they are a leader. Here are two examples (poem and collection of words) using the name JASON:

POEM	WORDS
Joining friends	**J**oyful
Around a campfire	**A**mbitious
Singing songs	**S**incere
Only to discover	**O**bservant
No one but he knows the words	**N**oble

Enrichments

1. Provide art supplies and encourage kids to creatively decorate their individual or group posters. Hang the finished products on the wall or a public bulletin board or in a display case.

2. Have small groups develop a simple script and play using their acrostic as the springboard. Remind them to create characters who are leaders or who represent the words they chose to include in their acrostic. Have them come up with a conflict or problem that the leader must deal with or solve. To build public speaking skills, ask that every person in the group have a speaking role. Have each small group write the script and perform their play for others.

LEADERSHIP
Acrostic

L _____

E _____

A _____

D _____

E _____

R _____

S _____

H _____

I _____

P _____

LEADERSHIP
Letters

L _____

E _____

A _____

D _____

E _____

R _____

Icebreakers and
WARM-UPS

Icebreakers are typically some of the first activities you'll conduct with a newly forming group. These activities allow individuals to introduce themselves to others in fun, low-risk ways. They promote rapport and relationship-building and help set the stage for future activities and discussions that will teach specific leadership topics or prompt deeper understanding of other people and ideas.

Icebreakers also can be useful as stand-alone activities when you want to fill time with a focused activity but don't necessarily want to deliver an in-depth lesson plan.

BALLOON
Train

The object of the activity is for the group to travel from a start line to a finish line using the balloons to stay connected like a train. Working together to keep the team connected by balloons teaches kids leadership skills related to communication, teamwork, choosing and following a leader, patience, and setting and achieving simple goals.

Time: 5–10 minutes

Age: Grades K–6

Group Size: No limit

LEADERSHIP LEARNING CONCEPTS

- Communication
- Patience
- Qualities of Leadership
- Teamwork

SUPPORTING STANDARDS

This activity supports content standards in Health and Physical Education (see pages 9–14 for details).

MATERIALS NEEDED

- balloons of various sizes, one less than the total number in the group
- large garbage bag
- space to move around
- simple obstacles and/or playground equipment (see Variation on page 27)

Getting Ready

Blow up the balloons and store them in a large garbage bag (or two, depending on the number of balloons). Move desks, tables, and chairs to the side of the room to create a large space for the group to move around. If you prefer, keep the room in its original state prior to explaining the activity, allowing an additional five minutes for the group to move the chairs and tables to the side of the room. Identify the start and finish lines where you want the group to travel as a train. This distance can vary from 20 feet (for K–2) to 100 feet (for third grade and up), either in a straight line or weaving in different directions. This session also can be conducted outside.

Activity

Introduce the activity before passing out the balloons (they can be distracting!).

Have kids imagine their group is a train. Point out the start and finish lines and let them know they must travel that course while remaining connected to each other using the balloons. Other than the person they choose to be at the front of the train—their locomotive—each of them will hold a balloon between themselves and the person in front of them without using their hands. If the balloon drops, the entire train returns to the start. Once the group reaches the finish line without dropping a balloon, their "trip" is over.

There is one other rule: Using static electricity to "stick" the balloons to themselves or each other isn't allowed. To get started, have students choose the person they want to serve as the locomotive. Urge them to work together to make this decision based on who they think will best guide the train. Is it someone who speaks the loudest, or someone who is the most patient, or someone who listens well to others? Or maybe they just want to ask for a volunteer.

Once any questions are answered and a locomotive has been selected, pass out the balloons. The person who is the locomotive won't have one. Have everyone else line up behind that person, and after "connecting" their team, encourage the locomotive to guide the train.

Step aside and allow the group to master their path. Keep track that the balloons keep the train connected for the entire activity.

Talk About It

Using terms your students will understand, ask questions like the following to help explore the leadership learning:

- How did you choose the person to be your locomotive? What was it like to be the locomotive?
- How well do you feel your group worked together?
- What did the group do in order to succeed?
- Share words that describe how people showed leadership in this activity. (Some examples of phrases that describe leadership behaviors you needed to succeed at this activity could be: *cooperate, teamwork, patience,* and *speaking up.*)

For kids third grade and up, consider asking these questions in addition to the previous ones:

- How do you talk with people on your team or in a group when they fall behind or need to keep up with the group?
- Was there any temptation to cheat and use static to hold the balloons to your bodies? Why did or didn't you do this?

Variation

If getting from point A to point B is easy for the group, create a simple obstacle course or ask them to set different challenges as a group, such as going farther, having to climb over some large rocks or through a playground set, or beating a certain time when traveling a particular path.

SESSION · SESSION · SESSION · SESSION

4

LINKED

In the context of testing a new balloon toy, teams learn to work together, overcome limitations and obstacles, seek opportunities to be resourceful, and maximize success as a group. This simple activity teaches more about leadership and communication than one might initially anticipate.

Time: 10–15 minutes

Age: Grades K–6

Group Size: No limit

LEADERSHIP LEARNING CONCEPTS

• Teamwork

• Communication

• Resourcefulness

SUPPORTING STANDARDS

This activity supports content standards in ELA–Speaking and Listening, and Health and Physical Education (see pages 9–14 for details).

MATERIALS NEEDED

• balloons of various sizes

• large dark garbage bag

• space to move around

Getting Ready

Blow up balloons and store them in a dark colored trash bag. Have plenty of balloons blown up, with a minimum of one balloon for each group of three or four kids. Move desks, tables, and chairs to the side of the room to create a large space for the group to move around. If you prefer, keep the room in its original state prior to explaining the activity, allowing an additional five minutes for the group to move the chairs and tables to the side of the room.

This session can be conducted outside, as long as obstacles and sharp vegetation or sticks are out of the way of balloons that may touch the ground.

Activity

Divide the large group into smaller groups of three or four, depending on overall group size (see page 5 for suggestions on how to divide the larger group). Allow two minutes for the small teams to come up with a name before explaining the activity.

When each team has a name, explain the activity by describing an imaginary scenario like this:

Your teams have been chosen to test a newly invented balloon toy. It's fun to play with unless it hits the ground. Hitting the ground turns it into an instant lead weight—no fun at all!

Give each group a balloon. Make sure groups are spread out from one another so they have room to move around. To test the new toy, have them join hands and work to keep the balloon up in the air and off the ground. Everyone must keep their hands joined the entire time. Provide a few minutes for practice, allowing them to use any body part they want to keep the balloon up.

Well done! Now that you've practiced, the toy manufacturer wants you to test the balloons further. Within your group, choose a "caller." Caller, you will call out different body parts the group must use to touch the balloon as well as keep helping the group test the toy. The parts called are the only things everyone can use to keep the balloon off the ground. Unless your caller says to use your hands, keep them joined the entire time. I will say "switch" when it's time for the caller to choose a new body part. Good luck!

Allow teams to select their caller. Once teams begin, call "switch" every 10 to 15 seconds. Teams could start with hands only, move to heads only, followed by elbows only, knees only, and noses only. Depending on your group, you may want to point out what body parts are appropriate. See Variations at the end of the session for additional ideas.

Talk About It

Using terms your students will understand, ask questions like the following to help explore the leadership learning:

- Was this activity fun? Why? What skills did each of your teams need to keep the balloons from touching the ground? (For example, teamwork, communication, problem solving, or creative thinking.)

- What was it like to be your group's caller?

- How did your group succeed even though you needed to keep your hands joined together?

- How well did your team communicate?

- Is there anything you would change about how your team worked together?

For third grade and up, consider asking these questions in addition to the previous ones:

- Can you think of any group projects or team experiences where you felt like the project would have been easier if you weren't "held back" by others on your team?

- How do you talk with others on your team or in a group about keeping up with the rest of the team?

If conducting Variation 1, also ask:

- Was there ever a time when you felt like the caller was unaware of how his or her instruction would affect the entire group? (For example, maybe the caller called a complex series of body parts that confused people or was hard to follow.)

- In real life, how would you deal with having a leader (like a teacher, coach, or youth group leader) telling you to do something that seems overly complicated?

Variations

1. For groups capable of greater physical movement and challenges, select random callers from the group and instruct these leaders to create body-part combinations for the groups to follow—for example "head-hand-elbow"—meaning the head hit must be followed by a hand hit, then an elbow hit, returning again to the head. Encourage them to make up different sequences (some could be hard, such as nose-heel-shoulder). After one leader has called a sequence or two, select a new leader midway into the sequence. Have that leader make a new call. Repeat a few times to give several kids a chance to be the caller.

2. In addition to the "Talk About It" prompts, include observational questions about the different leadership styles demonstrated by each caller.

CONCENTRATION

Good leaders, it can be said, tune in to what's happening around them and build better teams by paying attention to others. In this activity, kids work against an opposing team to identify and remember ways that the other team changes their outward appearance. Despite the simplicity of this activity, developing skills related to observing differences beyond what's obvious also can be emphasized.

Time: 10–15 minutes

Age: Grades K–6

Group Size: Unlimited number of equal-sized groups of 8–16

Note: For some groups, particularly younger groups or groups in which social interactions have recently been an issue, this activity can be the springboard for a discussion on paying attention to social cues and interactions (like how people get along) in the classroom or on the playground.

For third grade and up, it can be used as a reminder of the importance to include and support others, especially those being bullied or excluded by social clique behaviors.

LEADERSHIP LEARNING CONCEPTS

- Teamwork
- Observation Skills
- Discernment

SUPPORTING STANDARDS

This activity supports content standards in ELA—Speaking and Listening, Social Studies, and Service Learning (see pages 9–14 for details).

MATERIALS NEEDED

- dry-erase board or chart paper and marker

Activity

Divide the large group into two equal teams and arrange the teams into lines facing each other. Explain that each team should look closely at the other, trying to memorize as many details of the physical appearance of the other team as possible. Then one team will turn around while the other team gets 30 seconds to change 10 things about themselves (for example switch jewelry, change hair style, untie shoelaces, trade shoes, move watches to different arms, trade clothing, and so on). All changes need to be things that are in sight—that is, people won't trade socks or move items from one pocket to another.

When the unchanged side turns back around, they get one minute to identify the first team's 10 changes.

After they identify all the changes (or time is up, whichever comes first), it is their turn to make changes while the first team turns away. Proceed with one minute for the second team to identify the 10 changes.

Before each round, give the teams a couple minutes to make a strategy. After each round, tally the number of changed items each team notices on a dry-erase board or chart paper.

Depending on the age and attention span of the group, you can take turns several times, adjusting the number or difficulty of things that are changed. Total the tally and declare one team the winner of the "Most Observant" team.

Talk About It

Using terms your students will understand, ask questions like the following to help explore the leadership learning:

- How did you decide what 10 things to change? Was it easy or hard to come up with exactly 10 things? Did you choose a leader to help?

- How easy was it to notice how others had changed? What changes were most easily missed? Why?

- What did you do to remember the changes you noticed?

- What happens when a friend (teacher, parent, coach) is trying to tell you something but you're paying attention to other things nearby?

- In real life, have you ever thought you saw or heard one thing, only to discover you were paying attention to the wrong or less important thing? Explain.

- Pretend you were walking down the street and witnessed someone running away from a bank. Later at night, there's a news report of a bank robbery at the bank at the exact time you walked past it. Do you think you'd be able to describe the person you saw running away? Why or why not?

- How do you decide what's important to pay attention to and what's not?

For third grade and up, consider asking these questions in addition to the previous ones:

- What can happen if you focus solely on one problem or task and don't pay attention to other things that seem unimportant at the time?

- How often do you notice others? How do you let others know you notice them?

- Do you think it is important for leaders to notice how others around them change? Why or why not?

Enrichment

Ask students to write about what they can learn from the changes they observe in others on a daily basis. Select a particular form of writing the assignment should take such as expository or explanatory, or even ask them to write an article that could be included in a newspaper for kids (real or not).

Extensions

1. Have kids keep track for one full day how well people pay attention to changes. Suggest examples such as: a street light changes from red to green, but the driver in the car at the front of the line is distracted; kids are playing on the playground and don't notice the bell ring to call them in; a kid in class feels down because no one commented on his or her new shoes. Remind them to watch what happens as soon as the change is noticed. Encourage them to consider possible consequences of missed chances (opportunities) that happen because someone isn't paying attention. Talk about what this has to do with leadership and being a leader (see above for a list of questions for third grade and up).

2. Have kids create an ongoing blog or use movie-making software to document the changes they notice around them on a daily basis. Another option is to take pictures of changes they notice and create a before-and-after PowerPoint presentation or Animoto video (www.animoto.com).

FAMOUS
Pairs

Without knowing what's written on an index card taped to their backs, kids try to find who has the match to the name, activity, or object written on that index card. This low risk interactive activity for all ages promotes an atmosphere of friendliness while also setting the stage to discuss deeper topics related to diversity and differences.

Time: 20–25 minutes, depending on group size.

Age: Grades K–6

Group Size: No limit, although even numbers work best

LEADERSHIP LEARNING CONCEPTS

- Getting to Know Others
- Tolerance and Diversity

SUPPORTING STANDARDS

This activity supports content standards in ELA—Speaking and Listening, Social Studies, and Service Learning (see pages 9–14 for details).

MATERIALS NEEDED

- index cards
- tape
- writing utensils

Getting Ready

Prior to starting the activity, write the names of objects, activities, or people that go together in pairs on separate index cards (see Sample Pairs list on page 34). For example, write "salt" on one card and "pepper" on another. Make as many individual cards as there are kids in the group, so you have half as many pairs as kids in class. No pairs (or individual words) should be repeated unless you have an odd number of kids in your class. In that case, select one pair and write two cards with the same half of a pair on it, and one with the other; or you can create triplets. Using the previous example, you would have two cards with "salt" written on it, and one with "pepper." There are also a few triplet examples on the Sample Pairs list. If you have a three-person "pair," explain how you have accommodated this before the activity commences.

Unless you want kids to make up their own questions when they're interviewing one another, develop a brief list of getting-to-know-you questions you want them to ask one another after becoming a pair. Examples might include:

- Where were you born?
- What are your favorite things to do? (Or what are your hobbies?)
- What three words describe you?
- Can you speak a different language?
- How many kids are in your family?
- How do you spend your free time?

You can also consider selecting questions from the list of Sample Questions from the Leadership Talk Show activity found on page 42.

Activity

Tape one card on the back of each person without letting him or her see what it says. Explain that you will give a "go" signal and students are to walk around, *asking only yes-or-no questions* to find out what is written on their back. Once they determine this, they are to find their matching partner.

Once pairs successfully find each other, ask that they sit down and do an interview (general get-to-know-you questions), finding out three to five interesting facts about each other. Invite pairs to tell the larger group who or what was on their pair cards, and to introduce the person who is their partner.

Variation

For third grade and up, have each person in the group brainstorm a pair and, without sharing their pair with others, write each partner of the pair on a separate index card. Because everyone is writing a set of pairs, you will end up with twice as many pairs as needed, so select only the number of pairs necessary. Collect the cards and proceed with the rest of

the activity. Remind kids to keep the pairs appropriate and relevant (you want to avoid negative stereotypes and/or inappropriate pairings—for example, beer and wine).

Enrichments

1. Write specific interview questions on the backs of each of the index cards before placing them on kids' backs. These questions can be unique to, or the same for, every pair. Once every pair is matched, have them turn their cards over and respond to the interview questions. To increase application to learning more about diversity, have questions focus on how things (people, beliefs, etc.) can go together well even when they might be very different. Simple questions or prompts such as "What's your favorite subject?" or "Tell me about your family," or "How do you spend your summer?" can open kids to talking about their similarities and differences. When everyone has spent a few minutes talking, have pairs introduce their partners to the rest of the group, sharing what they learned about them.

2. For fourth grade and up, bring depth to the activity by creating a lesson around differences in race, culture, religion, socioeconomics, etc., and how people learn to get along with those who are different from themselves. Discuss what happens when conflict arises because of these differences, referring to national and international current events highlighted in the newspaper, issues in your local community, or clique behavior in your school.

Sample Pairs

The pairs on this list are from a wide range of topics and interests in kid culture. If using pairs from this list, select the most relevant and appropriate pairs for your audience. For grades K–2, select straightforward pairs that require little knowledge of popular culture, movies, or literature. For third grade and up, select more challenging pairs or ones that relate to current trends and fads in their lives. If your community or setting has pairs that make sense (such as certain cultures, foods, languages, or pop culture references) create your own pairs, jotting them down for future reference.

Pairs

Salt/Pepper
Ketchup/Mustard
Mickey Mouse/Minnie Mouse
Right/Left
Romeo/Juliet
Dora/Diego
Jack/Jill
Barbie/Ken
Lewis/Clark
Bread/Butter
Milk/Cookies
Peanut butter/Jelly
Adam/Eve
Batman/Robin
Addition/Subtraction
Tacos/Burritos
Spaghetti/Meatballs

Pool/Lifeguard
Rain/Umbrella
Texting/Email
Tom/Jerry
Movies/Popcorn
Monkeys/Bananas
Dinosaurs/Fossils
Chalkboard/Chalk
Microsoft/Apple
Vampires/Bats
Cats/Dogs
Trees/Grass
Happy/Sad
Mouse/Trap
Hamburgers/Hotdogs

Triplets

Hat/Mittens (Scarves)
Up/Down (Diagonal)
Coffee/Tea (Hot chocolate)
Katniss/Peeta (Gale)
Percy Jackson/Annabeth (Grover)
Soap/Water (Bathtub)
Bert/Ernie (Cookie Monster)
Harry Potter/Ron Weasley (Hermione Granger)

SESSION · SESSION · SESSION · SESSION

7

ALL ABOUT US
Bingo

This interactive activity encourages individuals within the group to learn about each other in a one-on-one way. Kids talk to everyone in their group, trying to gather signatures to fill in boxes on a diversity "bingo" card. Each box describes a different characteristic children in the group might represent.

Time: 25–45 minutes

Age: Grades K–6

Group Size: No limit

Note: For third grade and up, consider using the Variation (page 37), which allows your group to discuss and fill in their own characteristic boxes using a blank, customizable form. This option requires more time and a deeper or more sophisticated understanding of tolerance and diversity.

LEADERSHIP LEARNING CONCEPTS

- Tolerance and Diversity
- Self-Disclosure
- Getting to Know Others

SUPPORTING STANDARDS

This activity supports content standards in ELA—Speaking and Listening, Social Studies, and Service Learning (see pages 9–14 for details).

MATERIALS NEEDED

- fine-point markers or colored pencils, a different color for each participant
- "All About Us" handout (page 41 for grades K–2; page 39 for third grade and up)
- Optional (for fifth grade and up): Blank customizable "All About Us" handout (page 40; see Variation on page 37)

Getting Ready

Make a copy of the "All About Us" handout for each person, or prepare and copy your own handout using the customizable form. For third grade and up, place the markers or colored pencils in a central location, accessible to everyone. For younger kids, you may want to minimize distractions by passing out the markers or colored pencils instead of asking each kid to choose one from a box or table.

Activity

Pass out a copy of the "All About Us" handout to each child. Ask everyone to choose one marker or colored pencil to use for the entire activity. Before anyone writes on the form, explain the goal of the activity:

> **Everyone in this room comes from a different background. You each use different words to describe all the characteristics that make you unique. For example, you might be: an only child, an athlete, left-handed, able to speak more than one language, a vegetarian—or many other things!**

You might also describe yourself to illustrate the lesson, saying something like:

> **Take me, for example. I'm Latina, Christian, bilingual, an oldest daughter, and a football fan. These are all descriptions of the groups I'm part of along with other people who are Latino, or Christian, or bilingual, or oldest daughters, or fans of football.**

Explain that kids will walk around the room and meet as many others as possible, one person at a time. When they meet a person, they will say hello and, if necessary, introduce themselves to one another. Then they'll ask which box on the "All About Us" handout describes each other. Each time they meet someone, they can sign just one box on the person's sheet, and the person can sign just one box on theirs. Then they'll each move on to other people. Say:

> **Consider all the boxes that could describe you, and try to write your name in a different box on each sheet instead of signing the same box over and over. This may mean thinking of things that others may not know about you. Please use the same marker or pencil throughout the activity, so at the end you'll be able to clearly recognize everyone by the color of their name.**

Answer any questions and explain any of the boxed descriptions your students may struggle with, then begin. After everyone has connected with others in the group and the handouts are completely filled in, bring the group together to discuss the experience.

Talk About It

Have everyone hold up their sheets and look together at the different colors that show up in each of the boxes. If you see interesting patterns—such as person A and person B signed their names in different boxes, yet also share similar ones—comment on this and encourage kids to look for other things that stand out as they look at everyone's handouts (such as how the sheets all appear to be "color coded" as a way to describe everyone in the group). It may be helpful to go around the room, having kids say what color marker they used and talk about what boxes they liked signing in most and why.

Using terms your students will understand, ask questions like the following to help explore the leadership learning:

- What did you learn about the ways people describe themselves?

- Are there any groups that nearly all of you belong to? (In what boxes did almost everyone write their name?)

- In what ways is everyone in this group the same? In what ways are you different? What can you learn from these similarities and differences?

- Did you sign a box that others didn't know described you? If so, what box? How did it feel to show that information about yourself?

- Did you sign any boxes more than once? Why?

- Were there any boxes that a lot of kids signed to describe themselves but that you didn't? If so, how does it feel not to be part of that group?

- Have you ever been in a group where you were different from everyone else? Did you act differently than you would normally? Why or why not?

- When people in a group are very different from one another, what can leaders do to help people get along?

For fifth grade and up, consider asking these questions in addition to the previous ones:

- How do you make those who are different from you feel welcome—for example, when a new kid comes to your school or joins your sports team? If others don't feel welcome, what can you do to change this?

If conducting the Variation, also ask:

- What are some words or groups that you identify with but that you didn't write on anyone's sheet? Why didn't you write these down?

Variation

For fifth grade and up, use this variation if you have a group that has a strong grasp of diversity or may benefit from having time to think deeply about who they are as individuals as well as how they represent themselves to the outside world. Rather than using the Bingo card preprinted with descriptions, make copies of the blank sheet on page 40. You will have kids write words or descriptions in each box to represent the different communities they belong to or values that are important to them. In this case, introduce the activity similarly to the way described on page 36, but replace the last script section with the following script:

The list of groups you belong to could be very long, and it will be unique from the list of groups to which others belong. What you write in your boxes could be things that others notice immediately, such as the color of your eyes or hair, or things that people would have to ask in order to learn this about you. This handout is blank so you can write in descriptions of the different groups represented by everyone in this room.

You are going to walk around and connect with as many people in the room as possible, one person at a time. When you meet a person, say hello and, if necessary, introduce yourselves to one other before asking:

"What characteristic or group do you belong to that is very important to you or describes you in some way?"

Write the name of a group or description and then sign your name in one box on the other person's sheet. The other person will do the same on your sheet. The remaining boxes on your sheet stay empty until you encounter and introduce yourself to a different person. At that point, ask this new person the same question listed above.

Here are some examples of what students might write in the boxes:

- the name of their particular culture

- the kind of music they like

- special holidays they celebrate

- the name of a different language(s) they speak

- that they are a vegetarian

Use examples that are relevant to the age and setting of the group you're working with.

Encourage students to write something different on each sheet instead of writing the same information about themselves over and over. They should use the same marker or pencil throughout the activity, so at the end everyone will be able to clearly recognize each person's group/descriptions by the color of the writing.

Conduct the activity as explained in the Activity section.

Extensions

1. Conduct a brief lesson on diversity and what it means. This lesson can be done either before or after the main activity. Because children have different perceptions, both from other kids and from adults, of what diversity means, focus on presenting the topic in real-life, relevant ways. Some sources for age-appropriate lessons are:

   • Anti-Defamation League (www.adl.org)

   • Diversity Council (www.diversitycouncil.org)

   • Teaching Tolerance (www.tolerance.org)

2. Display the finished "All About Us" sheets on the wall or board so others can view and read them when the group gathers again.

3. Create an interactive "Who Are You?" bulletin board in a public location. Have students title the board and creatively express all of the words that reflect who they are—as individuals and as groups. Attach a few markers to the board (using string and tape to keep the markers in place), with instructions nearby encouraging passers-by to answer the question "Who Are You?" If the board is written on with negative terms, allow time for kids to "fix it" and to talk about how they feel seeing people destroy it.

ALL About Us

Instructions: Sign your name in only one box on the sheets of other kids in the group. Try to write your name in a different box on each sheet you sign.

I am not afraid of the dark	I have never been camping	I am the youngest in my family	I like to volunteer and help others	I have a special talent that others don't have
I am an only child	I have lots of sisters and brothers	I was born in this city or town	I celebrate a unique holiday	I like to swim
I have a pet	I am a girl	My religion is important to me	I like to cook	I know or have known all of my grandparents
I am a boy	I have been to a different country	I am or have been a Girl Scout or Boy Scout	My favorite subject is math	_____ is my favorite holiday
I am bilingual	I have a family member who is a soldier	I like to play outside	I am the oldest kid in my family	I play a musical instrument
I enjoy reading	I am left-handed	I like _____ (style) music	I like to try new things	I spend my free time reading

ALL About Us

Instructions: Ask each person you meet to write the name of a group he or she belongs to or a word or phrase that describes him or her in one box and sign his or her name. Do this until all your boxes are filled.

ALL About Us

Instructions: Sign your name in only one box on the sheets of other kids in the group. Try to write your name in a different box on each sheet you sign.

I am not afraid of the dark	I have never been camping	I am the youngest in my family	I like helping others
I am an only child	I celebrate a unique holiday	I like to swim	I have a pet
I am a girl	I like to cook	I know or have known all of my grandparents	I am a boy
I have been to a different country	I speak more than one language	I have a family member who is a soldier	I like to play outside

SESSION · SESSION · SESSION · SESSION

8

LEADERSHIP
Talk Show

Kids (and adults) of all ages struggle with focused listening and taking turns during conversation. This activity helps kids learn to "clear the clutter" in their heads, preparing them to listen better (for example, in a classroom) and improving their ability to engage in the subtleties of conversation as they get older.

Because half the group speaks at the same time during this activity, the room can sound chaotic. Even so, when half the participants are speaking, the other half is probably listening better than they would in a quieter setting.

Time: 20–40 minutes, depending on group size and age

Age: Grades K–6

Group Size: No limit, although even numbers work best

Note: For K–2 kids, select or design interview questions that are concrete, clear, and simple in meaning (such as, "If you were a type of dog, what would you be and why?"). You can preselect questions on the handout for kids to use or write your

own. Kids third grade and up begin to interpret more abstract questions ("Describe a time when you felt really proud about something someone else said or did.") and can "read between the lines" of a question, which allows them to respond with their own flair.

LEADERSHIP LEARNING CONCEPTS

- Communication
- Getting to Know Others

SUPPORTING STANDARDS

This activity supports content standards in ELA—Speaking and Listening (see pages 9–14 for details).

MATERIALS NEEDED

- "Sample Leadership Talk Show Questions" handout or a projection of the questions on an interactive whiteboard
- enough floor space to allow two equal lines to sit facing each other

Getting Ready

Make copies of "Sample Leadership Talk Show Questions," half as many as the total number in the group. If conducting the activity using Variation 1, set the room up as indicated. Otherwise, create enough floor space to accommodate the number of participants.

Activity

Divide the group into two equal-sized groups. If you have more than 20 participants, divide the group into four equal-sized groups. Have each set of two groups sit in lines facing one another, a short distance away from each other. One goal of this activity is to get quiet kids to come out of their shells and louder kids to tone it down. Based on what you know about each child in the group, mentally note which side will begin as Talkers and which side you want to begin as Listeners. With that in mind, pay attention to how you organize the lines, taking into consideration who's sitting beside or across from one another and if friends might be a distraction. Allow enough time so that everyone participates in both roles.

Explain that one side will begin as Listeners and the other side will begin as Talkers. Indicate which side is which, then distribute the "Sample Leadership Talk Show Questions" handout to each Listener. Tell them not to share it with the Talkers. Instead, they are to ask the Talker across from them *one* question on the list and then listen to what the Talker says. They can choose any question they want, but they are not to list all the questions for the Talker to choose from. The Talkers will have one minute to share their answer with the Listener. Say:

> **Listeners, I know it's hard to wait your turn to talk and not ask questions or interrupt. But your job is to be silent and pay attention to listening. You can offer encouragement like smiling and nodding to the Talker. Other than that, just concentrate on what the other person is telling you.**

Have them begin. When the one minute is up, give a signal and have Listeners and Talkers shift one seat to the right. Everyone will end up with a new partner. Those at the end of each row can rotate to the opposite row—a Talker becomes a Listener, and a Listener becomes a Talker. After each switch, Listeners ask their new Talkers one question, and the Talkers take one minute to answer. You may want to allow the Talkers to ask their Listener for a different question if they have already answered the one that the Listener selects.

Keep time and have kids move every minute until everyone has been both a Listener and a Talker at least once. Monitor the group to make sure Listeners ask only one question and are listening rather than prompting Talkers further (or interrupting). Allow at least 10 to 15 minutes for this activity and group discussion.

Talk About It

Using terms your students will understand, ask questions like the following to help explore the leadership learning:

- What did you like better—being a Listener or being a Talker? Why?

- What was your favorite question to ask? Why?

- What was your favorite question to answer? Why?

- Was there any answer someone gave that you really liked or found interesting? Explain.

- When you were a Listener, was it hard to keep from interrupting? What was it like to have to stay quiet?

- What did you learn during this activity that might help you listen better?

- Is it ever hard to focus on a parent, coach, or someone else who is giving you directions? Explain.

When guiding the discussion, you may want to share that sometimes *you* think people talk too fast, or it takes time to think about or process what someone has said before being able to answer or act on it. If time allows, explore age-appropriate developmental issues (such as comprehension, processing, and framing) related to talking and listening.

For third grade and up, consider asking these questions in addition to the previous ones:

- When you were a Talker, was it hard to answer without saying "ummm," laughing, or getting sidetracked? How can you clear the "clutter" in your mind to listen and talk more clearly?

- When you were a Listener, how was your listening different from how you normally listen?

- When you were a Talker, did you ever wish the Listener would encourage you by asking a question? When you were a Listener, did you ever want to help the Talker along? When and why?

- Have you ever been in a group or on a team when others didn't listen to you? Why do you think they didn't? What can you do differently to get others to pay attention?

Variations

1. Rather than using the floor for seating, arrange chairs or carpet squares in two lines facing each other. This can help keep things organized if the group has a tendency to get squirrely or distracted when sitting in undesignated spaces.

2. Divide the large group into groups of two or three kids each. Give each group at least three questions (or one for each person in the group). Ask each small group to select a "host" and one or two guests. Have them role-play as if they are hosting a television show, with each person taking a turn as host and guest to ask and answer a question. Remind each host that his or her role is to give the guests the ability to answer the questions fully, even if they want to cut in or add their opinion. Make sure every child has a turn in each role. Allow small groups a few minutes to practice before inviting each group to the front of the room to present their "conversation." Have the audience rate the conversation for how well each interviewer listened to the guests. Discuss Talk About It questions, with slight modifications to format as relevant.

3. If you'd like the activity to emphasize kids getting to know one another rather than active listening/communication skills, divide the large group into pairs of kids. Have pairs find a quiet place to sit before taking turns asking and answering questions from the list, reminding pairs to allow equal time for both members to answer the questions.

Sample LEADERSHIP TALK SHOW Questions

If you were a piece of furniture, what would you be and why?

If you were a household appliance, what would you be and why?

What would you do if you knew that the world would end in a week?

What was your best vacation ever and why?

If you could be an automobile, what would you be and why?

If you could cure one disease, which one would you cure, and why?

If you were a dog, what type of dog would you be and why?

Describe a time when you felt really proud about something someone else said or did.

Describe a time when you felt like you did something really well.

If you were a wild animal, what animal would you be and why?

If you could be a body of water, what would you be and why?

What's your favorite color? Name three reasons why and three things that come in that color.

People say that you look a lot like _____. How do you like that comparison?

If your life were made into a movie, what actor or actress would you want to play you?

If you could change one thing about yourself, what would it be?

If you had a month to travel someplace other than where you live, where would you go?

If you could design a (video or board) game, what would you call it and how would it be played?

If you could only drink one beverage for two weeks, what would it be?

Do you think of yourself as older or younger than you really are? Explain.

What is your favorite TV show and why?

If you could be a cartoon character, who would you want to be and why?

If you could ask anyone in the world a question, who and what would you ask?

What is your favorite food? Give three reasons why.

What would you like to be when you grow up?

Describe a dream you can still remember clearly.

SESSION · SESSION · SESSION · SESSION

9

BLANKET
Ping Pong

The object of this game is to earn points by causing a ping pong ball to roll off of the other team's side of a sheet or blanket, by raising and lowering the sheet as needed. As each team works together to prevent the ping pong ball from falling off the sheet to the ground, they learn how to work together, communicate, and balance multiple things happening at once.

Time: 10–15 minutes

Age: Grades 3–6, for eye-hand coordination reasons

Group Size: An unlimited number of groups of 6–10 (which will be divided into two competing teams of 3–5) can do the activity at the same time, using one blanket per group.

LEADERSHIP LEARNING CONCEPTS

- Teamwork
- Communication
- Problem Solving
- Qualities of Leadership

SUPPORTING STANDARDS

This activity supports content standards in Math and Health and Physical Education (see pages 9–14 for details).

MATERIALS NEEDED

- bed sheet or blanket, one for each pair of teams
- ping pong balls or other very lightweight balls, up to three per sheet or blanket that will be used
- space to move around (enough for each pair of teams so that teams are able to avoid bumping into one another)

Getting Ready

Move desks, tables, and chairs to the side of the room to create a large space for the group to move around. This session also can be conducted outside, as long as obstacles are out of the way.

Activity

Divide a larger group into groups of 6 to 10 kids of varying heights, if possible, then have each group divide into two teams of three to five members.

In this game, each team holds one end of the bed sheet or blanket and tries to roll the ball from its side of the sheet to the other. Each team's goal is to keep the ball from falling off its side of the sheet and to try to make it roll off the other team's side. A team gets a point each time it's able to get a ball to roll off—not bounce off—the sheet on the other team's side. Games will go for five minutes.

After explaining this basic setup, give teams a few minutes to strategize. Then position small teams on opposite ends of the sheet, having them hold it above the ground. Drop a ping pong ball in the middle of the sheet, say "go," and allow the game to begin. Remind the players to avoid "launching" the ball off the opposite side, as they will be very inclined to do so. If you have multiple pairs of teams going at the same time, you'll need to move around the room, serving as referee when necessary.

When time is up, call the game(s) and determine the winning team(s).

Talk About It

Using terms your students will understand, ask questions like the following to help explore the leadership learning:

- What skills did teams need to win points (for example, teamwork, communication, problem solving)?

- Were there any skills your group was missing (like not working together or losing focus)?

- Did anyone step up to become the leader for your team? Why or why not? If so, how did that person become your group's leader? If no one served as leader, do you think it would have helped to have a leader?

- What was it like to try to get the ball off the other team's side of the sheet while still trying to protect your side?

- How did it feel if the ball fell off the sheet right next to you?

- Did you use the original strategy your team discussed, or did you change your approach during the game? Explain.

If applicable, for kids placed into preselected teams:

- Would being able to choose your own team have affected your group's success? Explain.

Variation

You may conduct this activity as a cooperative, instead of competitive, initiative. For this approach, you still divide small groups into pairs of teams. The goal shifts from trying to get the other team's ball off the sheet to trying to keep as many ping pong balls on the sheet without falling. After starting the game, allow time for the teams to stabilize one ball on the sheet before dropping another ball onto the sheet. So that they aren't simply standing still, give them different commands to opposite team members that impact the sheet's movement (for example, "Billy, squat down, and Alicia, stand on your toes").

MARTIAN
Names

The activity is effective, easy, and fun to use at your group's first meeting. It allows kids to introduce themselves in a creative manner, while establishing a positive and warm group atmosphere. Kids write their names backward (in "Martian language") and then explain to the group what their name means. This silly approach allows kids to comfortably share a little about themselves without much risk.

Time: 25–35 minutes, depending on group size

Age: Grades 3–6

Group Size: No limit

Note: This activity can be used with grades K–2, but some younger kids may lack skills in letter formation, spelling, and reading, so you may need to write the names for them and help them practice pronouncing their Martian names.

LEADERSHIP LEARNING CONCEPTS

- Getting to Know Others
- Self-Disclosure (low-risk)
- Creative Thinking

SUPPORTING STANDARDS

This activity supports content standards in ELA—Speaking and Listening and ELA—Language (see pages 9–14 for details).

MATERIALS NEEDED

- markers
- 8½" x 11" colored paper

Getting Ready

To assist with explaining the activity, create your own "Martian name" sheet ahead of time and determine the meaning of your name in Martian language. If you are stuck, see the two examples on the next page of names converted to Martian, both in writing and meaning.

Activity

Pass out a piece of paper and marker to each participant. Create and tell a story to set up the activity, such as this:

> **You have just landed on Mars and need to introduce yourself to your Martian tour guide. Language on Mars is the complete reverse of ours. This means your name is the same, only backward: last name first, first name last, and both spelled backward, letter by letter. In addition, every name on Mars describes something special about the person who has that name. For example, my Martian name is _____, which means _____.** (Hold up the name sheet you prepared prior to conducting the activity.) **On your sheet of paper, write your name as it would appear on Mars. Practice pronouncing it. Think about the special meaning of your Martian name and get ready to share it with everyone in the group.**

To help kids come up with a meaning for their name, encourage them to consider what's important to them—special quotes, something they are good at, unique personal characteristics, cultural values, or other interests. Here are some examples:

- Sarah Jones becomes "Senoj Haras," which means "likes doing artwork and playing with my dog."

- Javier Martinez becomes "Zenitram Reivaj," which means "a loyal friend who loves playing soccer."

Talk About It

When kids have finished writing their names, go around the group and, one at a time, have them hold up their name sign, introduce themselves, and explain their name's meaning. In addition, have kids introduce their actual (Earth) names and say one or two other things about themselves. If you are using this activity at a point where kids in the group are just getting to know each other, you may consider asking additional simple, low-risk questions like these:

- What about this class (club, activity, camp, group) are you most excited about?

- What are you nervous about?

- Is there anything else that you'd like others to know about you, such as a favorite activity or person in your life, that you didn't share with your Martian introduction?

If space allows, hang up the sheets on a bulletin board or wall and leave them there for a few meetings to keep the group atmosphere friendly and warm. Otherwise, using glue sticks, have kids stick their name sheets onto one of their class folders or take the sheet home.

Understanding LEADERSHIP

This section of activities emphasizes what it means to be a leader and how to recognize leadership in others. Group members continue to build relationships and develop vocabulary related to leadership. In addition, these sessions help kids gain greater self-awareness about their own leadership talents and how to get others to recognize these talents.

These activities begin building critical thinking skills around leadership and being a leader. Therefore, it is most effective to conduct these sessions after kids in the group have developed a level of rapport with one another and have a basic grasp of the characteristics of leaders and leadership. While older students may think and share more deeply during discussions, the activities in this section are generally low risk.

Contains modifications for students transitioning to middle school

SESSION · SESSION · SESSION · SESSION

11

FUTURE
News Makers

In this warm-up activity, kids draw fictitious magazine covers featuring themselves. This activity helps students reflect on their potential for being leaders. Some of the covers might be funny, others more serious. Along with opening up and creatively expressing their future visions of themselves, kids also hear about the personal interests and goals that are important to others around them.

Time: 45–60 minutes (with discussion)

Age: Grades K–6

Group Size: No limit to group size

Note: When conducting this activity during a limited time frame, you may wish to divide larger groups into smaller ones of 10 to 12. This way everyone gets a chance to share their magazine cover, especially if you have kids who really enjoy drawing and creative design.

LEADERSHIP LEARNING CONCEPTS

- Values
- Qualities of Leadership
- Role Models and Mentors
- Creative Thinking

SUPPORTING STANDARDS

This activity supports content standards in ELA—Speaking and Listening, ELA—Writing, and Service Learning (see pages 9–14 for details).

MATERIALS NEEDED

- 8½" x 11" colored paper
- markers, colored pencils, or crayons
- Optional: magazines and/or Web magazine pages (displayed on an interactive whiteboard or accessed on individual devices) to show as examples

Getting Ready

Collect materials and create your own magazine cover ahead of time to share as an example.

Activity

Distribute the colored paper and markers (or colored pencils, crayons) to each person. Ask everyone to concentrate on her or his piece of paper while you describe a scenario. During this time, say:

> Years from now, you're looking at the cover of a magazine. It shows a successful leader in the world. The person on the cover is you. You're famous for doing something special and amazing like discovering a cure for a certain disease or inventing something new. Most magazines covers include a title, headlines, and pictures, but you can design yours anyway you want. Be sure to include your name somewhere on the cover.
>
> Here are some examples:
>
> - "Virgil Gomez Discovers New Comet!" on *Star Gazer*
> - "Meet the Parrot Lady—Jennie Smith Starts a Sanctuary" on *Animals Today*
> - "Book Lover Maris Yee Donates Collection" on *Library Archives.*
>
> You don't have to be a splendid artist to make your point!

Explain that students have 15 to 20 minutes (or longer if your setting allows) to design a personal magazine cover. Their magazine can be one that actually exists or is imaginary.

If kids need more guidance, show a few contemporary magazine covers, and add:

> Take a look at a few sample magazine covers. The headlines describe certain people or discoveries. So, what might make *you* the person someone is writing about? What could you have done to deserve recognition?
>
> Here are some questions that might help you imagine your magazine cover:
>
> - What are some of your favorite things to do right now?
> - What do you think you might be when you grow up?
> - How do your friends and family see you? What do they say you're good at?
> - What matters to you (big or small)?
> - What do you really care about? How do you want to make a difference in the world, or at your school, or in your city?

When everyone is finished, go around the group one at a time and have kids stand, introduce themselves, and show their covers. Encourage them to describe their covers and why being a leader in the way described is important to them. At a minimum, provide an opportunity for everyone to introduce themselves even if they don't share a lot about their cover.

Talk About It

In addition to talking about the messages magazine covers send about the people on them, lead a discussion about the difference between a leader and a celebrity. Kids third grade and up will be able to discuss these concepts in more abstract ways, such as incorporating examples from the news or who's currently popular, and discerning between leaders and celebrities (which may or may not overlap in different examples).

Ask kids what they think of each other's covers. Using terms your students will understand, ask questions like the following to help explore the leadership learning:

- What was surprising about all the ways people see themselves in the future?
- How do you think it would feel to really see yourself on the cover of a magazine? Explain.
- Do you ever take time to think about yourself in the future? Why or why not?
- Do you think that if someone is on the cover of a magazine, they must be a leader? Why or why not?

For third grade and up, consider asking these questions in addition to the previous ones:

- What's the difference between a leader and a celebrity?

- How often have you seen people on magazine covers or websites because they are celebrities who've done something troublesome—or attention-getting—and not because they have done something positive for the lives of others? What do you think about this?

- Should celebrities be thought of as leaders? Why or why not?

- Do you find it easy or difficult to view yourself as a leader? Explain.

- Do you think a person has to do something really big or life-changing to be a leader? Why or why not?

- Who are some leaders who have made dramatic discoveries or done something that has made an important impact on the lives of others, but may never have made it on the cover of a magazine?

Variations

1. Rather than designing a magazine cover, have kids draw a website home page. Encourage them to come up with a website name and URL, and include a menu of pages that describes the contents of the website.

2. For a more involved project, use GlogsterEDU (edu.glogster.com) or your school district's safe Google Site (sites.google.com) to have students create an interactive poster, website, or document that includes text, photos, videos, graphics—even music. Or have students use Pixton (www.pixton.com) to create a comic strip or graphic story about their future accomplishments.

Extensions

1. Ask kids to collect recent magazine covers—either in paper form or displayed from the Internet on an interactive whiteboard—that show the people who currently affect trends in society. During your next session, post the covers around your space where everyone can see them. Invite kids to stand by their magazine cover and describe the message they get from what's written or who's photographed on the cover.

2. On a sheet of chart paper or on an interactive whiteboard, have kids brainstorm ways celebrities use their popularity in good ways to inspire others. On another sheet, have kids brainstorm ways leaders can learn from how celebrities market themselves to gain attention. Explore whether kids think if leaders began marketing themselves "like a rock star," they would be doing a good thing or bad thing as role models.

SESSION · SESSION · SESSION · SESSION

12

LEADERS
in My Life

Using a list of 10 qualities or leadership characteristics, kids identify people they know personally who demonstrate these leadership qualities.

Time: 30 minutes (with discussion)

Age: Grades K–6

Group Size: No limit

LEADERSHIP LEARNING CONCEPTS

- Qualities of Leadership
- Role Models and Mentors

SUPPORTING STANDARDS

This activity supports content standards in ELA—Speaking and Listening, ELA—Language, Social Studies, and Service Learning (see pages 9–14 for details).

MATERIALS NEEDED

- "Leaders in My Life" handout (page 57 for third grade and up, page 61 for K–2)
- Optional: "Leaders in the World" handout (page 59 for third grade and up, page 63 for K–2) if conducting the Variation on page 56
- dry-erase board or interactive whiteboard (for jotting notes during brainstorming)

Getting Ready

Begin this activity by having kids verbally brainstorm words and descriptions that come to mind when they hear the words "leader" and "leadership." Write them on the board to keep track of all ideas. After the brainstorm is complete, discuss the wide range of leadership qualities. If you have already conducted the Defining Leadership activity on page 18, instead of another brainstorm, ask students to recollect the words they discussed during that session. After identifying words, you might say:

As you can see from brainstorming, a lot of things make people leaders. Every person has the potential to be a leader. Today we're going to think about qualities we see in leaders as well as how others see you as a leader. On your handout

is a list of 10 common leadership qualities. As you read through the list, think of people close to you—your mom or dad, grandparents, neighbors, friends, coaches, youth group leaders, cousins, siblings, or others—who demonstrate each of the leadership qualities. Write a different name on each line.

Depending on your group's reading level, you may choose to read each quality aloud or allow enough time for kids to silently read the list. Encourage kids to read the entire list before writing any names. After everyone has read and understands all of the qualities, have students write the name of a person they know on each line.

Talk About It

Start your discussion by asking different kids to use their own words to interpret each quality. Prior to guiding a general discussion, invite each child to share who he or she named for a few qualities and one or two reasons why.

Then, using terms your students will understand, ask questions like the following to help explore the leadership learning:

- How can you let people know the ways you consider them to be leaders?

- What qualities from this list describe you? Explain why you picked these qualities.

- Based only on the 10 qualities listed on the handout, how can you become a better leader?

Variation

Instead of having kids consider individuals in their lives, ask them to consider widely known leaders. This less-personal approach allows kids to gain the leadership learning at a somewhat superficial level because qualities of leadership tend to be easier to identify in well-known leaders. Conduct the activity as described, however, make and pass out copies of the "Leaders in the World" handout (pages 59–60 for students in grades 3–6 or pages 63–64 for students in grades K–2). Change the last paragraph of the script to reflect your interest in having them list well-known or popular leaders.

Complete the Variation in the same manner as described for the original activity.

Ask these questions in addition to the Talk About It questions:

- (If applicable): Several of you named the same person for the same quality. What does this tell you about how others view the person as a leader?

- What are some qualities of well-known leaders that are not on this list? Name the leaders and describe the qualities they have.

LEADERS in My Life

Write the name of **a person you know** (dead or alive) who fits each leadership description. Write a different name on each line.

Makes Good Choices _____

This person is a leader because he or she knows how to make well-thought-out decisions, follow the rules, and make choices in life that lead to good consequences.

Kind _____

This person is a leader because she or he is kind to others, helpful, empathetic (can understand other people's feelings), and treats other people the way she or he would want to be treated.

Role Model _____

This person sets a good example for others to follow, works hard at reaching goals, and acts in ways that are admirable. This person demonstrates many of the leadership descriptions on this page.

Responsible _____

This person is a leader because he or she can be relied upon to get things done. "DWYSYWD" is his or her motto (Do What You Say You Will Do)!

Trustworthy _____

This person is a leader because she or he is honest. This person is trusted by other people and is someone known for doing good things.

There's more!

LEADERS in My Life (continued)

Respects Others _____

This person is a leader because he or she never puts down other people, uses good manners, and treats others as if everyone is equal—no one is better than the next person. If another person is being treated unfairly, this person will do something.

Creative Thinker _____

This person is a leader because she or he comes up with new ideas when others are stuck or can't solve a problem. Instead of doing things in the same old boring way, this person looks for cool new things to do and see and try, and makes others want to do the same.

Calm and Reassuring _____

This person is a leader because he or she knows how to stay calm during all kinds of situations. Even when others may be worried or anxious, this person stays focused, on task, and in control—so other people stay calm, too.

Inspirational _____

This person is a leader because of who this person is, how this person does things, or what this person has overcome in life. She or he motivates me and makes me want to try my hardest and be my best.

Stands Up for Others _____

This person is a leader because he or she treats everyone as important. If other people are being picked on, put down, or bullied, this person confidently stands up and speaks out, even when others won't. He or she roots for the underdog.

LEADERS
in the World

Write the name of **a well-known person** (dead or alive) who fits each leadership description. Write a different name on each line.

Makes Good Choices _____
This person is a leader because he or she knows how to make well-thought-out decisions, follow the rules, and make choices in life that lead to good consequences.

Kind _____
This person is a leader because she or he is kind to others, helpful, empathetic (can understand other people's feelings), and treats other people the way she or he would want to be treated.

Role Model _____
This person sets a good example for others to follow, works hard at reaching goals, and acts in ways that are admirable. This person demonstrates many of the leadership descriptions on this page.

Responsible _____
This person is a leader because he or she can be relied upon to get things done. "DWYSYWD" is his or her motto (Do What You Say You Will Do)!

Trustworthy _____
This person is a leader because she or he is honest. This person is trusted by other people and is someone known for doing good things.

There's more!

LEADERS in the World (continued)

Respects Others _____

This person is a leader because he or she never puts down other people, uses good manners, and treats others as if everyone is equal—no one is better than the next person. If another person is being treated unfairly, this person will do something.

Creative Thinker _____

This person is a leader because she or he comes up with new ideas when others are stuck or can't solve a problem. Instead of doing things in the same old boring way, this person looks for cool new things to do and see and try, and makes others want to do the same.

Calm and Reassuring _____

This person is a leader because he or she knows how to stay calm during all kinds of situations. Even when others may be worried or anxious, this person stays focused, on task, and in control—so other people stay calm, too.

Inspirational _____

This person is a leader because of who this person is, how this person does things, or what this person has overcome in life. She or he motivates me and makes me want to try my hardest and be my best.

Stands Up for Others _____

This person is a leader because he or she treats everyone as important. If other people are being picked on, put down, or bullied, this person confidently stands up and speaks out, even when others won't. He or she roots for the underdog.

LEADERS
in My Life

Write the name of **a person you know** (dead or alive) who fits each leadership description. Write a different name on each line.

Makes Good Choices _____

This person thinks before doing anything that is unsafe or might get him or her in trouble. This person follows the rules and stays on task.

Kind _____

This person is very nice and helpful, and does not hurt others' feelings.

Role Model _____

This is someone I want to be like. This person is a hard worker and never gives up.

Responsible _____

This person always gets things done. She or he can be counted on.

There's more!

LEADERS in My Life (continued)

Trustworthy _____

This person always tells the truth. He or she does good things for others and never lies or makes things up.

Respects Others _____

This person is polite and uses good manners. She or he tries to make sure others are treated fairly.

Creative Thinker _____

This person uses his or her imagination to come up with new ideas. If people are having problems, this person is good at figuring things out.

Calm and Reassuring _____

This person is peaceful and not hyper. She or he stays on task and helps others stay calm, too.

Inspirational _____

This person makes others feel really good about themselves when he or she is around. This person cheers on others and says things like "good job." He or she makes me want to try my hardest.

Stands Up for Others _____

This person doesn't let people be bullies or pick on others. If people are hurting others, this person will try to stop them. She or he will get help if needed.

LEADERS
in the World

Write the name of **a well-known person** (dead or alive) who fits each leadership description. Write a different name on each line.

Makes Good Choices _____

This person thinks before doing anything that is unsafe or might get him or her in trouble. This person follows the rules and stays on task.

Kind _____

This person is very nice, helpful, and does not hurt others' feelings.

Role Model _____

This is someone I want to be like. This person is a hard worker and never gives up.

Responsible _____

This person always gets things done. She or he can be counted on.

There's more!

LEADERS in the World (continued)

Trustworthy _____

This person always tells the truth. He or she does good things for others and never lies or makes things up.

Respects Others _____

This person is polite and uses good manners. She or he tries to make sure others are treated fairly.

Creative Thinker _____

This person uses his or her imagination to come up with new ideas. If people are having problems, this person is good at figuring things out.

Calm and Reassuring _____

This person is peaceful and not hyper. She or he stays on task and helps others stay calm, too.

Inspirational _____

This person makes others feel really good about themselves when he or she is around. This person cheers on others and says things like "good job." He or she makes me want to try my hardest.

Stands Up for Others _____

This person doesn't let people be bullies or pick on others. If people are hurting others, this person will try to stop them. She or he will get help if needed.

SESSION · SESSION · SESSION · SESSION

HANDPRINTS*

This activity encourages participants to think about how others "touch" (influence) their lives in positive ways. After tracing the outline of their hands, kids write names or words describing people who represent certain qualities in each of the fingers. This is a simple way to help kids identify role models from an early age. This can be a meaningful activity to conduct at the end of an organized leadership experience or as part of the middle school transition.

Time: 25–45 minutes

Age: Grades K–6

Group Size: No limit

Note: You may have to coach younger kids (such as grades K–2) on the meaning of the phrase "touch." See the script for a list of ideas on how people may touch their lives. Older kids may want to go into more detail about how people have touched their lives, so allow up to 45 minutes.

LEADERSHIP LEARNING CONCEPTS

- Role Models and Mentors
- Getting to Know Others
- Values

SUPPORTING STANDARDS

This activity supports content standards in ELA—Writing and Service Learning (see pages 9–14 for details).

MATERIALS NEEDED

- chart paper
- construction paper
- masking tape
- markers or crayons
- Optional: scissors, hole punch, yarn or twine (see Enrichment on page 67)

Contains modifications for students transitioning to middle school

Getting Ready

Draw the outline of a hand large enough to fill a piece of chart paper or construction paper. Number the fingers one through five, with the thumb being number one and the pinky finger number five. Within the fingers, write these five statements:

1. A person you admire (either close to you or well known) and why

2. Name of someone who you learn a lot from (for example, a coach, friend, sibling, or cousin)

3. Someone your age who you think is a good leader

4. Words you might use to describe someone you think is a role model

5. The word(s) you want people to use when describing you (consider words that come to mind when you think of leaders or leadership)

Hang the large hand in a visible location where kids can easily see it while doing their handprints. Also, place the construction paper and markers or crayons in an area accessible to all.

Activity

Have kids write their name at the top of a sheet of construction paper before placing one hand on the paper and tracing an exaggerated outline of that hand (larger than their real hand). Encourage them to space their fingers apart so that each one is clearly separated from the others.

Starting with the thumb, have participants label the fingers with the numbers one through five in exactly the same configuration shown on the sample poster. (This is for consistency as they share what they've written in each finger.)

Explain that in life, some people make an impact on us—that is, they "touch" us in some way. Lead a discussion about the term "touch" and the ways a person might touch our lives. For example, someone who has touched your life might be someone who:

- has changed your life for the better

- motivates you or keeps you going when you get down on yourself

- supports you during tough times

- cheers you on

- you want to be like

Say:

When you're young, you might not notice these touches. But as you get older, you'll recognize them when given a chance to think about it. Just as your handprints remain on the things you touch, so do other people's "touches" remain with you.

In the individual fingers of their handprint, ask kids to write or draw their responses to the statements on the sample poster. Allow five to ten minutes for the students to do this. Once everyone has filled in their hands, bring the group together to share and discuss the handprints.

Talk About It

Older, more mature kids will likely share more deeply than younger kids because they better recognize why and how someone is important in their life, and how they want to be able to touch others as they get older.

Using terms your students will understand, ask questions like the following to help explore the leadership learning:

- What are some ways people have made a difference in your life?

- How do you find friends who are positive role models (for example, they don't get in trouble, they stay on task, and they do the right thing)?

- What kind of leader and role model do you want to be? (In other words, when someone talks about you, how do you want them to describe you?)

- Do you think others see you as a good role model and/or leader? If not, what can you do for others to see you this way?

For third grade and up, consider asking these questions in addition to the previous ones:

- What are some ways the people who've impacted (or touched) your life are the same?
- How would you like others to think of your impact on their lives?
- What makes a person's impact most memorable?
- Is there anyone you wish would reach out and touch you in some way? What can you do to let this person know how you feel?

If conducting this at the end of a program or leadership experience, or as a middle school transition activity, you may want to ask:

- How have people in this group touched you? How can you let them know how you feel about that?
- When you are in middle school, how will you find friends who are positive role models and help you become the best person you can be?
- How can you make choices in your own life that also make a positive impact on the lives of others?
- What activities can you get involved in (after this program/experience OR in middle school) that will allow you to reach out and touch the lives of others?

Variations

If using this activity for closure, write these statements in the fingers:

1. The person in this group you look up to and consider a good role model.
2. Someone in this group who has made a positive impact on you (helped you through tough times, cheered you on, given you good advice, helped you become a better person).
3. A person in this group you hope to have in another activity or class, or you hope will grow as a friend.
4. A person in this group you enjoyed getting to know or think you could still learn a lot from.
5. The leadership trait or personality characteristic you most want people to remember about you.

Enrichment

Have kids cut out their hand tracings. Punch a hole in both the thumb and pinkie finger of each hand. Cut a piece of yarn or twine that's long enough to weave through the holes of all the hands to create a garland of handprints to display. Working together, have kids weave their hands onto the string and hang the completed garland along a wall or across the room.

SESSION · SESSION · SESSION · SESSION

14

LEADERSHIP
Treasure Hunt

Unlike a scavenger hunt, this activity has small groups of kids work together to uncover leadership clues about their team. As you ask a series of questions, kids share information about themselves while finding out more about others. The activity is a good way to introduce how leadership looks different in every person.

Time: 35–45 minutes (depending on group size)

Age: Grades 3–6

Group Size: Unlimited number of equal-sized groups of 3–5

LEADERSHIP LEARNING CONCEPTS

- Qualities of Leadership
- Communication
- Tolerance and Diversity
- Getting to Know Others

SUPPORTING STANDARDS

This activity supports content standards in Social Studies and Service Learning (see pages 9–14 for details).

MATERIALS NEEDED

- "Leadership Treasure Hunt Statements" handout (page 70)
- "Leadership Treasure Hunt Score Sheet" handout (page 71)
- writing utensils

Getting Ready

Make one copy of the "Leadership Treasure Hunt Statements" for yourself. There are 16 statements on the list and room to write four additional statements, for a total of up to 20. Write any questions of your own and then select 10 to 15 questions total that are most applicable to your group (or that reflect specific things you want them to learn about each other in this activity). Number the statements on your sheet in the order you read them. This way,

68

everyone refers to the same statement during the scoring process.

Divide the large group into smaller teams of three to five members. Make enough copies of the "Leadership Treasure Hunt Score Sheet" so that every small group gets one score sheet.

Activity

Pass out a "Leadership Treasure Hunt Score Sheet" and pen or pencil to each team. Ask teams to identify a scorekeeper who is responsible for tallying the points throughout the activity. Explain the hunt like this:

You're going on a leadership treasure hunt. The hunt is for information about people in your group. I am going to read a list of statements, and after each one, you will talk with your team to find out who matches that statement (they have that quality or they have done that thing). Your team earns one point for every member who matches. Be honest in answering. The scorekeeper needs to tally the score for each statement and then tally the overall score for all of them.

Rather than just taking a vote and recording the tally, talk about each of the statements so you actually find out new things about the others in your group.

Answer any questions. If you are conducting this activity with a new group, take a few extra minutes to have members introduce themselves to their teammates.

Clearly read each statement, giving examples or answering questions as necessary, and moving on only when you think every small group has tallied their scores for a given statement. Plan to spend about 20 minutes asking the statements and allowing groups time to discuss them. When you've read your list, ask groups to calculate their overall score.

Because teams will keep a score based on an equal number of participants, the ideal is for every team to have the same number of members. If there is only a single "extra" person in the large group, invite that person to read the "Treasure Hunt Statements" aloud in place of you. If you have two or three additional people, create small groups with fewer members or have groups divide their final score totals by the number of members. You may determine other ways to assure fair distribution of points.

Talk About It

Bring together the large group, but have kids sit beside everyone in their small groups. Acknowledge the group that achieved the highest score. Using terms your students will understand, ask questions like the following to help explore the leadership learning:

- What did you learn about the other kids in your small group?

- Who can explain what "diversity" means? How diverse was your small group?

- Were there any statements that got a point from everyone on your team? Any that received no points? Explain.

- What statements caused the greatest discussion within your small group? Explain.

- How can the "treasure" you learned from this activity be used by our larger group in the future?

- What was the most interesting response in your group? Explain.

- What statements would you add to this treasure hunt?

Leadership Treasure Hunt Statements

If desired, write any alternate questions at the end of the list that follows before reading the list aloud to students. Then select 10 to 15 questions and number them in the boxes in the order you'll read them. Each team earns one point for *every* team member who "fits" the statements.

☐ You are involved in an activity outside of school such as a youth or scout group, a team sport, or an individual sport.

☐ You volunteer regularly.

☐ You're from a different cultural background. (Your small group can determine what "different" means.)

☐ You have a mentor.

☐ You have stood up to a bully (or a friend who's being pushy) for yourself or on behalf of someone else.

☐ You can correctly name the capital of our state (province).

☐ You speak more than one language.

☐ You have attended a leadership conference.

☐ You have been nominated or have run for a position to lead others (such as for a sports team, a scout or youth group, a school club, or another organized group).

☐ You plan to go to college.

☐ You play a musical instrument, sing in choir, or participate in dance or other creative art.

☐ You are usually the first person to introduce yourself when meeting someone new.

☐ You have won a contest or competition of any kind.

☐ You know the name of the current mayor, governor, and president (or other appropriate designations).

☐ You celebrate a unique holiday. (Your small group can determine what "unique" means.)

☐ You have written a letter to the editor, a Congress person, a mayor, a school principal, or another authority.

☐ _____
_____

☐ _____
_____

☐ _____
_____

LEADERSHIP TREASURE HUNT

Score Sheet

1. _____

2. _____

3. _____

4. _____

5. _____

6. _____

7. _____

8. _____

9. _____

10. _____

11. _____

12. _____

13. _____

14. _____

15. _____

Total: _____

WHAT I LOOK FOR in My Friends

The natural process children engage in when making and keeping friendships provides an avenue to build awareness about leadership characteristics and behaviors. This activity has kids rank the values they *want* friends to possess while also examining the type of friend they make.

Time: 30 minutes

Age: Grades 3–6

Group Size: No limit

LEADERSHIP LEARNING CONCEPTS

• Building Friendships

• Qualities of Leadership

• Decision Making

SUPPORTING STANDARDS

This activity supports content standards in ELA—Speaking and Listening, Health and Physical Education, and Service Learning (see pages 9–14 for details).

MATERIALS NEEDED

• "What I Look for in My Friends" handout (page 74)

• Optional: interactive whiteboard or document projector to project handout on larger screen

• writing utensils

Getting Ready

Make one copy of "What I Look for in My Friends" for each student.

Activity

Give every student a copy of the handout "What I Look for in My Friends." Ask everyone to find a spot in the room where they can focus on their own sheet and not be tempted to look at others' responses. Encourage friends to sit away from one another.

Explain the activity like this:

For the next 10 to 15 minutes, you are going to read through this list and select the top 10 qualities you look for in a friend. Lots of choices are on the page, so read through the entire list first, then go back to complete your ranking. If

you think any important behaviors are missing, write them on the blank lines at the end of the list and include them in your ranking. Please don't share your choices or talk with others, especially friends, while doing this.

When time is up, ask kids to gather as a large group again. Invite volunteers to share their list and any comments related to completing the handout in private. Because this activity may feel very personal for some kids, be certain to allow time for discussion.

Talk About It

Using terms your students will understand, ask questions like the following to help explore the leadership learning:

- Have you ever thought about the qualities you think are most important in your friends? What was it like to think about these?

- Are the qualities we want in friends similar to or different from what we expect of leaders? How so?

- Do you consider your friends leaders? If yes, what are some ways your friends behave as leaders? If no, what are some ways you think your friends could learn to behave as leaders?

- Has a friend ever done something that went against what you expected of that person? What happened?

- How do you handle friends who say or do things that hurt your feelings?

- Have you ever tried to control how a friend acts or what he or she does? How did that go for you? What happens when friends try to do this to you?

- How do you let your friends know what you appreciate about them?

- When your friends make choices that might put them in danger or get them in trouble, how can you help them? How is this like being a leader?

Enrichment

Select one child to tally everyone's top 10 rankings by placing a small mark in front of each statement on the handout whenever someone includes it in the ranking. (The tally keeper doesn't track who ranks the statement or whether the ranking is number 1, 2, and so on.) Take 5 to 10 minutes to track the rankings and then discuss the results. If creating a "Top 10" list, consider asking these additional questions to further explore the leadership learning:

- Which 10 statements showed up the most?

- What do these top 10 tell you about what you all expect from friends?

- How well do you feel you—as a friend—represent these top 10 statements?

- What does it mean if your friends have different qualities ranked higher or lower than you?

Extensions

1. Have children write a special letter to a friend. The letter can include their list of the top 10 things they look for in friends, with an explanation of how that person demonstrates these qualities. Have them decide when or if they want to give it to that person.

2. Have kids create a "Friendship Day" event. Organize activities and discussions that promote friendship, connections, and everyone being a leader to others. Kids can make and trade friendship bracelets, organize buddy activities between older and younger kids, plan playground activities that depend on people working together, and do other activities.

3. Have kids plan and lead "Mix It Up" activities to encourage widespread culture of friendship and leadership in their setting. Mix It Up at Lunch Day is an annual one-day event during which kids are required to eat lunch with someone new. Schools and communities sometimes do other activities to promote building new friendships and breaking down stereotypes (social, racial, language, etc.). To learn when Mix It Up at Lunch Day is scheduled each year and to get free resources and activities, visit www.tolerance.org/mix-it-up/what-is-mix.

WHAT I LOOK FOR
in My Friends

_____ Loyal

_____ Cares about me

_____ Follows rules

_____ Knows how to make safe choices

_____ Can make a decision

_____ Has his or her own opinions and views

_____ Won't talk about me behind my back

_____ Good at sports

_____ Good at school

_____ Goes with the flow, is flexible

_____ Is not an energy vampire (doesn't take more than she or he gives)

_____ Has a positive outlook

_____ Can see something good in everyone

_____ Confident

_____ Trustworthy

_____ Stands up for me

_____ Good listener

_____ Fun to be with

_____ Makes me laugh

_____ Can play with more than one friend at a time

_____ Enthusiastic

_____ Stays cool under pressure

_____ Keeps drama out of our friendship

_____ Open and honest

_____ Shares similar interests

_____ Likes having different interests

_____ Helpful

_____ Friendly and kind

_____ Talks about more than himself or herself

_____ Likes trying new things

_____ Can stand up for herself or himself

_____ Respectful

_____ Genuine and real

_____ Doesn't pressure me to do something I don't want to do

_____ _____

_____

_____ _____

_____

_____ _____

_____

Becoming a LEADER

Once kids begin learning leadership skills, they need opportunities to practice them. Becoming a leader requires using a combination of learned skills, which leads to action-oriented behaviors and critical thinking, which then leads to participating in informed conversations and making confident decisions. The sessions in this section provide young leaders a chance to practice the leadership skills they've learned (and are learning) within the context of thoughtful discussions with peers.

Contains modifications for students transitioning to middle school

CONNECTIONS*

Because this activity emphasizes vocabulary and communication, it provides an easy way to conduct leadership learning in the context of language arts. Part 1 has kids thinking of and defining leadership terms. Part 2 has kids organized in a circle, communicating their words to one another, and connecting to each other using a ball of yarn. The yarn is tossed across the circle until a symbolic leadership web is created.

Conducting this activity prior to the Egg Hunt activity on page 80 accomplishes two goals. First, kids become familiar with leadership terms and their definitions to use for describing their peers, and second, you create a list of words from which kids can choose when filling slips of papers to insert into eggs.

Time: Part 1: 30 minutes (depending on age)

Part 2: 15–30 minutes (depending on age)

Using Variation in place of Part 1: 15 minutes (depending on age)

Age: Grades K–6

Group Size: Groups of 8–36 (you can break the group into smaller groups for Part 2 if you prefer)

Note: For a more sophisticated version of this activity to conduct with older students (grades 5–6), you can conduct "The Web" activity on page 56 of *Teambuilding with Teens* by Mariam G. MacGregor, M.S. (Free Spirit Publishing, 2008).

LEADERSHIP LEARNING CONCEPTS

- Teamwork
- Communication
- Problem Solving

SUPPORTING STANDARDS

This activity supports content standards in ELA—Speaking and Listening and ELA—Language (see pages 9–14 for details).

MATERIALS NEEDED

- dry-erase board, chart paper & markers, or interactive whiteboard
- index cards, one for each word that will be used in the web
- dictionaries (optional)
- roll of string or yarn (ample amount)
- space to move around
- Optional: "Connections Sample Word List" handout (page 79) (for Variation)

*Contains modifications for students transitioning to middle school

Getting Ready

If using an indoor room, create a large open space by pushing chairs and desks to the edge of the room.

If conducting the Variation (page 78), make a copy of the "Connections Sample Word List" for each student or project it at the front of the room via an interactive whiteboard.

Activity

Depending on your time frame, you may conduct Parts 1 and 2 on the same day or during separate sessions.

Part 1. Ask kids to brainstorm a list of words that come to mind when they think of someone who is a leader. Have a volunteer write these words on the board. After you have collected more words than you have group members, have kids take turns selecting one word from the list. They can choose whatever word they want for whatever reason they want, and once it is picked it's unavailable to the other group members.

Pass out index cards. Have kids write their word on the index card along with a definition using their own language or using a dictionary. Ask that they not share their definition with others until told to do so.

For an alternate approach, see the Variation on page 78.

Part 2. Once everyone has chosen, written, and defined a word on an index card, ask kids to gather in a circle. If you have a large group, you might want to divide it into smaller groups so that the activity moves faster, although a large leadership web can be impressive to make and see.

Next, tell your class:

The words from your brainstorming and on your cards represent a lot of the characteristics and qualities this group believes are important for someone to be a leader. But when one person doesn't have all these qualities—or is trying to be a better leader—that's when you need a team. Today, you are going to form a team, and this (hold up the yarn or string) **is going to hold you together.**

Hand the ball of yarn to a person who will serve as the starting point. Ask that student to read his or her word and definition from the card. After reading, have the student toss the yarn to a person across the circle. Have that person read his or her word and definition, loop a finger around the yarn to hold onto it, and toss the yarn ball to a new person across the circle, and so on. When everyone has read his or her word and the yarn resembles a web, ask the group to keep holding onto the yarn and sit down if they are standing (still in a circle).

Talk About It

Explain that the yarn has created a web that connects everyone in the group. During discussion with kids in grades K–2, encourage the group to apply these words and the web to working together in every-day situations such as playing on the playground, following classroom rules, helping each other with projects, etc. For upper grades, relate this activity to additional everyday situations such as group projects, competitive athletics, cooperation on the playground, and role modeling for younger kids. Using terms your students will understand, ask questions like the following to help explore the leadership learning:

- What do you think about the web your group has created?

- What would happen if anyone from this team left the circle and let go of the string?

- What happens if one person in your group or on your team doesn't do what everyone else in a group expects of him or her?

- What word from this web do you think describes *you*?

- Can you think of friends or family members you'd use any of these words to describe? What will you do to tell them about the ways you think they're leaders?

- Would you like to have someone tell you you're a leader? Why or why not?

- What sorts of things (actions or behaviors) in our classroom (school, program, team) would make it impossible to keep this web together?

- Are there any behaviors or words you think are missing? How would having those additional characteristics or qualities as leaders make this group stronger?

Middle School Transition Questions

If you are using this activity with fifth- or sixth-grade students who will be heading into middle school, consider including these questions during the discussion:

- List the top 10 leadership words that you hope others use to describe you. Is there anything you could change about yourself so others would describe you that way?

- When you start new in middle school, what sort of web do you want to create?

- How do you deal with friends when they continually cause the web between you to disconnect or fall apart? What would you do if someone you're working on a project with does the same?

- How do you repair your web when you feel disconnected or discouraged by what is happening in your life at any time?

- Who can you count on to bring strength and leadership characteristics to areas where your skills might still need developing?

Variation

Instead of having kids brainstorm a list of words during Part 1, make one copy of the "Connections Sample Word List" (page 79) for each student and pass these out or project them via interactive whiteboard for everyone to see. The handout has four blank lines that you can use to fill in any words you'd like to add. Have kids select a word from the list. Pass out index cards and have kids write their word on the index card. Allow a few minutes for them to write a definition of the word on their own or using a dictionary. Ask that they not share their definition with others until told to do so.

CONNECTIONS
Sample Word List

Friendship	Role model
Trustworthy	Funny
Responsible	Sticks up for others
Truthful	Determined
Helpful	Smart
Happy	Motivating
Encouraging	Nice
Hard worker	Inspiring
Fair	Loyal
Fun to be around	Independent
Respectful	Keeps promises
Humble	Ethical
Creative	_____
Powerful	_____
Confident	_____
Positive	_____

SESSION · SESSION · SESSION · SESSION

17

EGG HUNT

Kids draw a slip of paper with another person's name, write leadership words or phrases that describe the person on the other side, and then place that slip of paper inside a plastic egg. Later, kids will search for and open the egg that has been written about them. Because this activity emphasizes giving positive feedback to others, it can be used as a meaningful activity for the end of a program or school year.

This session is best conducted when you have time after kids write on the slips when you can hide the eggs (like a scavenger hunt) before they search for them.

Time: 20–30 minutes (depending on group size)

Age: Grades K–6

Group Size: No limit

LEADERSHIP LEARNING CONCEPTS

- Qualities of Leadership
- Appreciating Others
- Feedback

SUPPORTING STANDARDS

This activity supports content standards in ELA—Language, ELA—Writing, and Service Learning (see pages 9–14 for details).

MATERIALS NEEDED

- medium-sized, two-piece plastic eggs (one for each student)
- slips of paper (approximately fortune-cookie size), large enough to write on
- writing utensils

Getting Ready

Write each child's name on five separate slips of paper. Place the slips into a basket or hat. On each egg, write one child's name and place the empty eggs in a line on a table where the names can be visible when the eggs are picked up.

For younger kids, you may want to provide a list of leadership words for them to choose from during the activity. You can use the "Sample Personality Adjective List" on page 118 or the list of words from the Connections activity on page 79 to guide kids in word choices. If using a word list, write the words on a dry-erase board or display them on an interactive whiteboard.

Activity

Have kids take turns picking five different name slips out of the basket or hat. If they pick their own name or the same name more than once, have them return those slips to the basket after they've picked five different slips (to prevent from picking them again). Ask that they not show their slips to anyone else.

Explain that on the blank side of each slip of paper you want them to write a leadership word that describes the person named on the other side. For younger students, you can refer them to the word list you have provided for inspiration, though they should not feel compelled to choose from that list if they have other ideas for a person they have drawn. If they want to write a collection of words or phrases, that is great, too. Have them sign their names under the comments they write. Once everyone finishes writing on their slips, ask that they go to the empty eggs, locate the five eggs with the names of their peers written on it, and put their slips of paper into the appropriate eggs. There will be multiple slips of paper in each egg. When everyone is done, collect all of the eggs into a basket.

When kids are out of the room (either the same day or on another day), hide the eggs around the room (or outside, in hallways, or in other class-rooms kids may enter around the building). At the time when you want them searching, invite kids to look around and find the egg with their name on it. Once everyone has found their egg, provide enough time for them to read the slips inside. You can allow privacy or invite kids to read their slips aloud and publically acknowledge what was written. See Variation for an approach that promotes public acknowledgment.

Talk About It

No further discussion is necessary with this activity, but if you are using it as a closure activity (at the end of a specific leadership experience), you may want to provide 5 to 10 minutes for kids to share what it meant to be part of the group or comment on what people wrote. Pay attention to include everyone in the group and make sure each member is recognized during the final discussion.

Consider these additional prompts:

- Does anyone want to say something to another person about what they wrote to you?
- Overall, what would you say about your experience as part of this group?

Variation

Instead of having kids find their own egg, have them search for and find an egg with someone else's name on it. Once all of the eggs are found, take turns having each person read aloud the name on the egg they found and what's written on the slips inside. Ask that the person whose name is read to stand in a spot where the person reading their attributes can see them and speak directly to them. Return the slips of paper into the egg after reading before passing the egg to the person.

WHAT'S IN A
Name?*

This activity explores the importance of first impressions. By having kids wear name tags that represent positive and negative characteristics alongside their own name, the "gut" reaction they experience can lead to particularly insightful discussion. When used during middle school transition sessions, this activity can be especially impactful because it helps tweens evaluate what type of first impression they hope to make when going to a new school (or meeting new students and teachers) at their middle school.

Time: 30 minutes

Age: Grades 3–6

Group Size: No limit

LEADERSHIP LEARNING CONCEPTS

• First Impressions

• Qualities of Leadership

SUPPORTING STANDARDS

This activity supports content standards in ELA—Speaking and Listening and Service Learning (see pages 9–14 for details).

MATERIALS NEEDED

• adhesive name tags ("HELLO, My name is"), three for each person

• markers

• tables, desks, and an open space that allows for chairs to be organized in small circles around them

• dry-erase board or interactive whiteboard

*Contains modifications for students transitioning to middle school

Activity

Lead a discussion about making first impressions. What kinds of things do kids notice about people the first time they meet them? Write a collection of responses on the board. Then ask what they think people notice about them the first time they meet them, and write their responses on the board.

Pass out three name tags and a marker to each child and explain that on the first one, they are to write the one characteristic they like least in other people—maybe they brag too much, are untrustworthy, make bad choices, or are lazy. Have kids select one or two strong words or phrases, not the *name* of a person, that describe qualities or actions they dislike in others. Allow a minute or two for this before asking them to put the name tag on their chest.

Say:

Look around at everyone's name tags. Think about the words on your tag as if they are a "label." How do you feel having this "label" on you, especially because the word describes behaviors, attitudes, or actions that bother you? When you look at the labels on others, does it make you think that person is like that? What might others be thinking when they see the label you're wearing? (Share)

As much as you may want to take this name tag off, I won't let you!

On their second name tag, have kids write the one characteristic they feel makes them stand out as a leader. Are they a good communicator, trustworthy, ethical, organized, or confident? Again, they should capture this characteristic in one or two strong words. Ask them to put this name tag on their chests on top of the first one. Say:

Cover up your first name tag—so no one sees that negative label underneath. Look around again. Look at your friends. Is this how you see them? Has your opinion changed when you don't see the negative hiding beneath a positive?

Allow for responses to these questions. Now, have students take their final name tag and write their name on it. Have them look at their name and think about the words they wrote on the previous two name tags.

Place this tag on top of the others. Or, if you feel more comfortable—less like you're hiding something—you may take off the others and really start fresh. How do you feel now? Does this name tag feel "heavier" or "lighter" than the first one you put on when we started?

Talk About It

After students share responses to the questions you ask during the activity, ask questions like the following, using terms your students will understand, to help explore the leadership learning:

- Which name tag did you like wearing the most? Least? Explain.

- What do you want others to think of when they hear or see your name?

- What are some important things you can do to make a good first impression? (Talk about clothing, shaking hands, eye contact, words they choose, behavior in public, and other things people do to make a good first impression.)

- What happens if you make choices or act in a way that gives others a different first impression than you were hoping to make?

- There is a saying that goes, "You're known by the company you keep." What happens if your friends act or talk or treat others in ways that make you look bad?

- Do you think people deserve a second chance to make a good first impression? Explain. Are you willing to give others a second chance? Would you want others to give you a second chance?

If this activity is part of the middle school transition, consider asking these questions in addition to the previous ones:

- When you enter middle school, what is the first impression you hope to make?

- What impression do you want middle school teachers to have of you? Is this the same or different from how you've been seen in elementary school?

- What can you do to keep others from getting the wrong first impression of you?

- How will you handle situations where others pressure you to do things or make choices that are out of character with who you are?

- Think about the impression people get of you from what you say online, including forwarded emails or texts and gossip. First, how do you make sure you send the right messages about yourself? Second, what can you do to overcome negative things people may believe about you, even if they've never met you in person? Third, what can you do to keep gossip and false comments about others from circulating?

SESSION · SESSION · SESSION · SESSION · N

19

EVERYDAY
Dilemmas*

This activity sparks thought and conversation to guide kids with how to handle difficult situations with confidence, ethics, and integrity. Depending on upbringing, outlook, and frame of reference from personal experiences, some kids may approach the discussion with a more absolute point of view: *There's a right and there's a wrong,* or *I would always do this, I would never do this.* Others will explore (and struggle with) the abstract "grayness" that comes with difficult situations.

Time: Varies

Age: Grades 5–6

Group Size: No limit, divide kids into groups of 3–4

LEADERSHIP LEARNING CONCEPTS

- Decision Making
- Ethics
- Values

SUPPORTING STANDARDS

This activity supports content standards in ELA—Speaking and Listening, Social Studies, and Service Learning (see pages 9–14 for details).

MATERIALS NEEDED

- "Sample Everyday Dilemmas" handout (pages 88–89)
- chart paper
- markers
- tape

*Contains modifications for students transitioning to middle school

Getting Ready

Determine how you will divide the larger group into smaller groups of three to four. Refer to page 5 for different methods for creating small groups.

Make enough copies of the "Sample Everyday Dilemmas" handout so that you can cut out dilemmas for each group to have one. See Variation for guidance on having kids write the dilemmas for this activity.

Activity

To introduce how everyone encounters tough situations in their lives, lead a discussion to define the meaning of the words *ethics*, *values*, and *dilemma*. Ask for suggestions about what kids think each word means, and fill in the discussion with information similar to the following:

- **Ethics** are rules and standards generally agreed-upon by society that help people decide what is right—or most right—in any situation, especially when there's no clear answer.

- **Values** are those beliefs, ideals, and things that are important to us, our family, our friends, or our group.

- A **dilemma** is a situation or question you face where you feel stuck between two difficult choices, or choices where one direction doesn't stand out as that much better than the other.

Follow this up by saying something like:

We all experience moments when we have to make difficult choices. When you're in a leadership role, decisions often call for balancing your personal ethics and values with the needs of your group. As an individual, you find yourself balancing similar things—that is, your values with the values of your friends or parents. A lot of difficult decisions are made by trusting our gut.

Ask the group what they think it means to "trust your gut." Kids might give examples of times they have trusted their gut. To wrap up the discussion, you might say:

If you are uncomfortable after making a decision—if it doesn't feel right in your gut—you may have acted unethically. When you use ethics to guide your decisions, you are less likely to make poorly thought-out decisions or decisions that have negative consequences for you and for others. You are less likely to try to find an excuse for why you acted the way you did.

Benjamin Franklin once said, "He that is good for making excuses is seldom good for anything else." Making decisions without making excuses (or feeling like you need to explain yourself) can be hard. But it is worth it to try making the "best" right decision at the beginning.

Sometimes making a decision means choosing between two equally difficult options. The "right choice" may not be perfect, but it's better than the other choice. These situations are called *dilemmas*. An example is choosing whether to speak up when you see a kid being picked on, even though others think he's "weird." If you defend the kid, you might be picked on, too, or labeled weird. If you choose not to defend the kid, you are letting him be hurt, and you may not feel very good about yourself. Making choices in these situations is easier when you can still respect yourself afterward and know you've acted the way you want to be throughout your life.

When making a decision, you probably don't ask yourself, "Is what I'm about to do ethical?" But you may have a feeling about whether you've made a good decision. Let's practice and learn more about making ethical decisions.

Organize kids into their small groups. Hand out chart paper, markers, and a different dilemma from the handout to each group. If you have more groups than dilemmas, write additional dilemmas and/or assign the same dilemma to more than one group. Allow 20 minutes for small groups to discuss and come up with decisions about how they'd deal with the situation they've been given. You can explain it like this:

In your small groups, discuss the ethical dilemma on your slip of paper. Talk about all of the things in the dilemma that could cause the decision to

be hard to make. Talk about the choices you can make and the pros and cons of each of the choices. What might happen as a result of your decision? Finally, make up your mind as a group what you will do. On the chart paper, write possible alternative choices, what ideas went into making your final decision, and your final decision. You have 20 minutes.

When all groups are done, post each sheet of chart paper where it's visible to all. Ask a spokesperson from each group to read their dilemma and present what their group talked about for the different alternatives, their final decision, and how they reached this final decision.

Talk About It

Using terms your students will understand, ask questions like the following to help explore the leadership learning:

- What are some ethical dilemmas you have faced?

- When dealing with ethical decisions in the past, what did you consider to help you decide?

- How often do you trust your intuition—your gut—when facing dilemmas or making difficult and ethical decisions?

- Think of a dilemma you faced alone that you wish you had handled differently. Is there anything you wish you knew *then* that you know *now*? Explain. How might that knowledge affect dilemmas you face in the future?

- Describe how you (or your group) may have dealt differently with any of the dilemmas we discussed today. Explain your decisions.

Middle School Transition Questions

If you are using this activity with students who will be heading into middle school, consider including these questions during the discussion:

- Do you think making decisions related to "sticky situations" in middle school will be complicated for you and your friends? Why? (Examples of sticky situations might include situations involving drugs and alcohol, cyberbullying, parties, academic and sports priorities, dating, relationships with parents and siblings, faith, and health choices.)

- How can you become better prepared for these sticky situations?

- When doing things with new friends, what steps can you take to make sure they know how you feel about the issues involved in these situations (that is, your values)?

- How can you express your values to others so that they know when they've "crossed the line" with you? (If necessary, ask kids to explain what "crossing the line" means to them. If anyone is confused about the term, provide an explanation.)

- Who can you turn to as you get older to help guide you in making decisions in difficult situations?

- How can you keep the lines of communication open with your parents, so you can call them when you need them?

Variation

Rather than use the dilemmas provided, ask everyone to write down a dilemma they've faced in their own life. Because some of their friends, or people everyone in the class knows, may have been involved in the dilemma, guide students to avoid including specific names. Put few limitations on what the dilemma is, other than to explain that to make a decision in the situation, they had to decide between difficult choices. Type, copy, and cut out these dilemmas and use them for the activity as described. During discussion, present the option for individuals to "claim" their dilemma and explain how they actually dealt with it in their life.

SAMPLE
Everyday Dilemmas

Not all of these dilemmas are appropriate for every setting. Please select the dilemmas from this sampling that best fit your situation and student audience. If these do not resonate with the kids with whom you work, identify dilemmas that do and create your own. Copy and cut so that each group can receive a slip of paper with one dilemma on it.

- ✂

While you are playing soccer on the field during recess, another group confronts your group, insisting that they want to play football on this field and that you have to stop playing soccer. Rules on the field say that when this situation arises, the two teams are supposed to split the field to share the space, even if it means groups have to play within half the normal size. You explain this to the captain of the other group, but that kid won't listen. "We *always* play football here," he says. You don't really want to go right to the playground monitor because she always says if there are problems, then the field is off-limits. What do you do?

- ✂

At a sleepover with your best friend, his parents are having guests over. Once the guests leave, a few half-full beers are left around. Your friend picks one up, smiles, and takes a sip, before offering the can to you. Your parents are at a late movie, so you are hesitant to call them. What do you do?

- ✂

Your older sister sneaks out regularly to meet up with her friends. You've always kept the secret for her. One night, when your mom finds your sister gone, she starts asking you what you know. Most of the time, this night included, you don't really know where your sister goes, who she's with, or what she does. You are really close to your sister and you don't want to betray her. What do you do?

- ✂

You've played on the same competitive sports team for four years. A new member joins the team and is getting all the attention. She's a good athlete, but she brags a lot. On the field, she never passes, makes fun of other team members, and talks back to the referees. The coach cheers her on because points count toward wins, except your team is starting to lose more games than ever, despite the new member's scoring ability. Other team members are skipping practices or messing around on the field and hogging the ball as well, just to get attention. What do you do?

- ✂

SAMPLE Everyday Dilemmas (continued)

- ✂

To complete a project for school, you are required to partner with two other people in your class. You think carefully before choosing your group, and for a while you are happy with how well your group is doing. On the day it is due, you realize that the person responsible for the essay completely plagiarized the material from the Internet by cutting and pasting from different websites. He changed a handful of words from the original articles, but nothing is written in his own words. You will all be penalized if this assignment is not turned in on time. What do you do?

- ✂

While visiting at the middle school you really hope to attend, you ask questions about how much homework is assigned and how well teachers get to know the students. The student leader you're with admits that she has cheated her way through a semester of algebra without ever getting caught. In fact, she says, some days the teacher has them do all of their work in small groups or on the computer, so he doesn't even know who is doing the work being turned in. This school is also your family's first choice pick for you. You are anxious and upset when your dad comes to pick you up. What do you do?

- ✂

Once a month for two years, you have gone to a youth group with friends. It is one of your favorite things to do. During the most recent meeting, one of the older kids with whom you've really bonded grabs your shirt and tries hugging you in an inappropriate way. After pushing him away, he says that if you tell anyone what just happened, he will be kicked out of the group and get into lots of trouble with his family. If you stop going to the group, your friends will definitely notice. What do you do?

(What if the inappropriate hug came in a different setting from someone else—for example, a coach, your parent's friend, a babysitter, an aunt or uncle, a cousin, a best friend's sister or brother?)

- ✂

You discover that a friend has been chatting online with someone she doesn't really know. This person says he's 14, attends the local high school, and is a friend of a friend. His profile includes a picture of a comic strip character, not a real person's face. You try to look him up in your brother's yearbook, but no one by that name is listed. When your friend IMs the boy with this fact, he tells her that he just moved to town this year. Your friend confides to you that she trusts him and plans to meet him at a nearby mall. You are really nervous that the person isn't really a kid. But if you tell an adult or ask your brother to find out, your friend may never talk to you again. What do you do?

- ✂

COMMUNICATION

Strong communication is an incredibly important life skill for a leader. Kids recognize early on who in their classes others listen to. They also connect quickly to those who listen well or empathize well with others. Leaders of all ages who are strong speakers and listeners find it easier to understand what ideas and issues are important to others, to get their own ideas across to others, and strengthen connections in their teams. Just like learning to play an instrument and make it sound good, learning to be a good communicator takes practice.

WORD LIST
Feedback

This activity provides a structured way for kids in K–2 to offer feedback and positive comments to others in a low risk way. Kids select from a list of positive adjectives and use these words to describe their peers. Build in time at the end for kids to read people's comments privately and acknowledge one another if desired.

Time: 20–30 minutes

Age: Grades K–2

Group Size: No limit

Note: The activity Back/Feedback on page 116 is an alternate version of this activity designed for grades 3–6. The "Sample Personality Adjective List" on page 118 is designed to be used with both activities.

LEADERSHIP LEARNING CONCEPTS

- Appreciating Others
- Feedback

SUPPORTING STANDARDS

This activity supports content standards in ELA—Writing and ELA—Language (see pages 9–14 for details).

MATERIALS NEEDED

- copies of a list of names of all kids in the group
- writing utensils
- dry-erase board or interactive whiteboard
- Optional: business-sized envelopes and stamps (for Variation)

Getting Ready

Type a list of the names of all kids in the group and make a copy for everyone. If you prefer, kids can use a sheet of notebook paper and write everyone's name in a list format. If you choose to do this, make sure no child is overlooked.

On the dry-erase board or interactive whiteboard, write a list of positive and encouraging adjectives used to describe people, being careful to select words familiar to your group. If you include more challenging words, take time with your group to explore definitions and usage in context. A sample list is on page 118.

Activity

Pass out a copy of the list of names to every child. Using the adjective list you've written on the board or are displaying on the interactive whiteboard, ask kids to choose an adjective to describe each person. Once they've selected the word, have them write why that adjective fits the person. For example:

Mai-Mai is thoughtful because she helps others when they are having problems.

Fergus is charming because he finds ways to make people smile even if they are sad.

Depending on reading levels and writing skills, allow plenty of time for all kids to finish their lists. When everyone is done, collect all of the lists. After the session, type a sheet with each child's name on it and the list of sentences everyone in the group wrote about them. Pass out each child's sheet to that child at the next session.

There is no need to conduct an additional discussion, unless you would like to provide an opportunity for kids to acknowledge specific comments written by others.

Variation

Instead of passing out the finished list to each individual, have kids write their mailing address on a business-sized envelope and turn it in to you. Mail each student a copy of the full list of names and adjectives after the group has finished being together (at the end of the school year or after campers return home).

BRICK
Houses

This activity is divided into two parts. During the first part, small groups work independently to build the largest block structure possible in a limited amount of time. They must complete this task without being able to talk with their own (or other) team members. Though not stated, the implication is that the groups are competing against one another. The second part requires the small groups to connect their different structures together, still following the same rules.

Time: 30 minutes

Age: Grades K–2

Group Size: Unlimited number of small groups of 3–5 members

Note: The House of Cards activity on page 107 is an alternate version of this activity designed for grades 3–6. The limited manual dexterity, patience level, and attention span of younger kids can make the original House of Cards activity challenging.

LEADERSHIP LEARNING CONCEPTS

- Teamwork
- Problem Solving
- Communication
- Creative Thinking

SUPPORTING STANDARDS

This activity supports content standards in Math, and Health and Physical Education (see pages 9–14 for details).

MATERIALS NEEDED

- large quantity of plastic building bricks (such as Legos or Mega Bloks), math manipulative blocks, or other cube-shaped, stick-together building items

Getting Ready

Depending on the space you use to conduct this activity, move any tables, chairs, or desks out of the way to create open floor space or together to create a large flat surface. Determine the method you'll use to divide the larger group into smaller teams so participants are not selecting their own teammates (see page 5). Place the plastic building bricks in a pile in a central location where all teams have easy access while building. The more teams you have, the more bricks you need.

Decide whether you want the small teams to a) build the tallest structure possible or b) use a certain quantity of building bricks (give each group the same amount) to build a tall structure using all (or as many as possible) of their materials within the time limit.

Activity Part 1

Divide the larger group into smaller groups of four to five members each and assign each team its own spot in the room, within reasonable proximity of one another in order to facilitate the second part of the activity.

Explain the activity like this:

In your small teams, you are going to use bricks to create the tallest structure you can from the ground up (or, *You are going to build the tallest structure you can by using all the bricks in your pile before the time is up*)**. You get 10 minutes to create your building. You may not use table legs, chairs, books, tape, paper clips, or any other items as support. There are two other rules. First, you can't communicate out loud with each other to accomplish your goal—this means no talking, grunting, humming, or other mouth sounds. Second, you can't draw or illustrate any of your ideas. You have only the set time to finish your structure; if it falls any time during those 10 minutes, start over. Everyone in your group has to be happy with the final structure.**

Take care to avoid setting up a competition between the teams; this tends to naturally occur and can be addressed in discussion. As teams start building, watch to make sure groups keep their structures freestanding, with no support from other objects or items. You may need to play a more active role monitoring the no-speaking rule, as young kids often hum, sing, or make other noises to try to communicate with one another. Let them know when they have two to three minutes left. After 10 minutes, call time and have teams step away from their structures.

Talk About It

Using terms your students will understand, ask questions like the following to help explore the leadership learning:

- What was it like to do this without talking or making any noise?
- How did you communicate?
- How did you know when everyone in your group was happy with the structure?
- How did your group deal with frustration? For example, if your building fell down, how did your group react and get going again?
- Did you feel like you were competing against the other group(s)? Why or why not?

Activity Part 2

After discussion, inform the separate teams that they will use more bricks and work together to connect all of the structures together. The no-talking rule still applies, as do all the other rules. The connecting structure must also be three-dimensional, with no other support systems. Again, the connection is not complete until everyone in the group (the entire group this time) is satisfied. Allow 10 minutes for teams to work together to accomplish this. Then call time, celebrate completion, and discuss.

Talk About It

Using terms your students will understand, ask questions like the following to help explore the leadership learning:

- What was it like to work with the entire group to accomplish a goal? How was it different from working with your small group?

- Did you still feel like you were competing with each other? Explain.

- How did your group communicate?

- How did your group know when everyone was happy and had achieved its goal?

- How would this activity have been different if you could have talked to each other?

- Did anyone act like a leader during this activity? If so, how did the person become the leader? Did having a leader help you achieve the goal? Explain.

- Was this like real life in any way? How?

Extension

Consider challenging kids to observe how people (themselves included) use nonverbal skills and rely on other strategies for communicating with others. If you ask them to do this, take 5–10 minutes the next time the group gets together to have them share what they observed.

SESSION · SESSION · SESSION · SESSION

22

COUNT OFF

With eyes closed, kids work together to complete a number or letter count off. This activity can be conducted in various renditions, allowing for alignment between leadership development and subject areas.

Time: 10–20 minutes (depending on group size)

Age: Grades K–6

Group Size: No limit

LEADERSHIP LEARNING CONCEPTS

- Active Listening
- Goal Setting

SUPPORTING STANDARDS

This activity supports content standards in ELA—Speaking and Listening, and Math (see pages 9–14 for details).

Activity

Spread the group of kids around the room in no particular pattern. If you are in a room with desks and tables, kids can remain seated. If you prefer, ask kids to spread out, standing in various locations around the room.

When everyone is in a spot, have them close their eyes. With eyes closed, explain the activity like this:

Today, you have one goal—to count from one to any number past ___, which is the total number of kids in this group, keeping your eyes closed. Sounds easy, right? There are a few rules to follow. First, every person must say at least one number. Second, a player can say more than one number, as long as those numbers aren't consecutive— like saying seven and then eight. Third, any time two or more people say the same number at the same time, the group has to go back to number one. Finally, other than saying the numbers, you cannot speak, not even to make a plan. You have as much time as you need. Ready? Go.

Allow the group to move at their own pace, reminding people to keep their eyes closed and bringing the group back to task if they get frustrated. Keep track of who has said a number, so you can be sure that everyone says at least one. When the goal is achieved, bring the group back together for discussion.

Talk About It

Give the group time to celebrate accomplishing their goal. Using terms your students will understand, ask questions like the following to help explore the leadership learning:

- How hard was it to do this without talking or making a plan?

- Did any clues emerge that helped you know when to speak?

- How did you feel when two people spoke at the same time and you had to start over? Do you think you would have this same reaction in a real-life situation that involved your group trying to achieve a certain goal? Explain.

- Describe the feelings you had during this activity. Did you notice any behavior about yourself that you had to overcome to contribute to your group's success? (Examples might include being more patient, staying quiet, letting others speak, or taking turns.)

- Can this activity teach you anything about being a good listener? If so, what?

- Why is it important for leaders to be good listeners?

Variations

Provide no planning time regardless of which variation you choose.

1. If the group easily masters this task, have them do it again, this time counting to the highest number the group can reach without getting frustrated.

2. If the group is large, divide them into teams and have the teams compete against each other. This is challenging because they can't always tell if the person speaking is from their own group or from one next to theirs.

3. Rather than counting off, conduct the activity by having the group say the alphabet in order.

4. To conduct this activity in the context of specific subject areas, have the "count off" revolve around certain topics, such as multiplication facts, words starting with the same letter, names of animals in a habitat, state or province names and capitals, countries, or geometry phrases.

THE ACCIDENTAL
Witness

People of all ages often have difficulty actively listening. A more complex version of the familiar "Telephone" game, this activity depends on, and reinforces the need for, listening fully and avoiding distracted listening.

Time: 20 minutes

Age: Grades K–6

Group Size: Best with classroom-sized groups, although can be conducted with any group size

LEADERSHIP LEARNING CONCEPTS

- Communication
- Active Listening

SUPPORTING STANDARDS

This activity supports content standards in ELA—Speaking and Listening (see pages 9–14 for details).

MATERIALS NEEDED

- stopwatch or digital watch
- "The Accident" handout (page 101 for grades 3–6 or page 102 for grades K–2)

Getting Ready

Make one copy of "The Accident." Prepare a short lesson on what active listening means to the group (see Activity).

Activity

Conduct a short lesson on the meaning of active listening—the simpler the better if you are working with young children. You might have kids brainstorm how they know someone is *truly* listening to them, or you may use an example about how you can tell if students are actively listening. You might consider including the following:

Sometimes when people give us directions or present a lesson, we aren't paying close attention to what's being said. Maybe we're daydreaming, or thinking about what we're going to do later, or

worrying about someone else, or thinking about what's for lunch. When this happens, it's easy to miss what another person is saying. Does that sound familiar? You're partly listening, but you're not listening fully—you're not *actively* listening. What does it mean to actively listen? What are some consequences of not actively listening? (Allow for responses.) **After our next activity, you'll have a better understanding of what it means to listen better.**

Select four volunteers and explain to the rest of the group that they are to quietly observe what takes place with the volunteers. Ask one volunteer to stay in the room. Send the other three to a nearby location (or just outside the room, with the door closed) where they cannot hear or see what is happening in the room.

Tell the first volunteer that he or she has just seen a terrible accident. This student is a "witness." Give the witness a copy of "The Accident." Allow the witness time to silently read "The Accident." For children who are just learning to read, you can read the story aloud to them while they follow along. If necessary, allow time to answer comprehension questions for them.

Let the witness know that he or she will be role-playing what happens after the accident by telling a police officer exactly what happened using the details from the story. If necessary, explain what it means to role-play. Younger kids may need more guidance; however, if you explain they are going to "act" like characters in a movie, they usually get it. Allow the witness to read the story from the handout but encourage him or her to pretend to tell it as if he or she had just witnessed it.

When the witness is ready, bring the second volunteer into the room. Assign this person the role of being a police officer who has just arrived at the scene of the accident. Prompt the witness to tell the police officer the story. Do not reveal that the police officer will have to repeat it.

When completed, retrieve the third volunteer and assign him or her the role of being a

medical professional who has arrived at the scene. Ask the police officer to tell the story to the medical professional.

Finally, bring the fourth volunteer into the room, and give him or her the role of being a news reporter. Direct the medical professional to tell the story. Then ask the news reporter to repeat the details to the audience (the observers) for the evening broadcast. When the final report is done, ask the witness to reread the original story for all to hear (or reread it aloud yourself).

Talk About It

Begin by asking the observers what they heard and saw with each new person entering the room.

- What happened with each retelling of the story?
- What did you think as you heard each person tell his or her version of the accident?

Next, ask the kids who took part in the role play for their views.

- What was it like to be told the story and then asked to repeat it to someone else?
- Would it make a difference if you knew before hearing the story that you would have to repeat it? Why or why not?
- How well do you feel you listened as you were being told the story? Did you use any tricks to remember the information? Did anything get in the way of your listening?

Ask these last questions of everyone in the group.

- How did the activity show the importance of being an active listener?
- How would you describe your usual listening style?
- What helps you pay attention and actively listen to what is being said?
- Why is it important for leaders to be good listeners?

The ACCIDENT

You witnessed a terrible accident. Below are the details of what happened. When the police officer arrives on the scene, you will tell him or her what happened (you can read from this sheet, but try not to sound as if you're reading). Speak expressively to convey your concern about what you saw or know. Do not give this sheet to anyone else.

A red two-door sports car was driving west on Leadership Avenue when a large St. Bernard dog ran across the lawn of a blue house and into the street in hot pursuit of a ball. The driver slammed on the brakes, sending the car into a 180-degree spin in front of oncoming traffic until it smashed into a silver old-model station wagon. The driver of the station wagon was a 50-year-old man with two poodles in the front seat. When pedestrians assisted the man from the vehicle, the poodles leaped out and ran after the St. Bernard. The man fainted in the center turn lane, so one of the pedestrians called an ambulance. One of the poodles suffered minor bite injuries on the right leg from the St. Bernard. A passing motorcycle killed the other poodle. Two teenage boys playing baseball at the time of the accident swear that the driver of the red car was going faster than the 25-mph speed limit.

The ACCIDENT

You just saw a big accident. Below are the details of what happened. When the police officer arrives on the scene, you will tell him or her what happened. You can read from this sheet, but try not to sound as if you're reading. Try to show your concern about what you saw. Do not give this sheet to anyone else.

A red car was driving on Leadership Avenue past the school when a large brown dog ran across the road. It was chasing a ball. The car's driver slammed on the brakes. A blue car smashed into the red car. The driver of the blue car was an old man with two little dogs in his car. When he got out of his car to check on the other driver, the dogs leaped out and ran after the large brown dog. The old man fainted when he saw his dogs had run away. Just then, a city bus screeched to avoid hitting the blue car.

SESSION · SESSION · SESSION · SESSION ·

24

SQUEEZE

Two teams line up separately and have a "squeeze race," passing a hand squeeze down their line with their eyes closed. The first team that completes the squeeze race, grabs a ball at the end, and tosses it into a bucket, wins.

Time: 15–30 minutes (depending on group size)

Age: Grades K–6

Group Size: No limit

LEADERSHIP LEARNING CONCEPTS

• Communication

• Patience

• Teamwork

SUPPORTING STANDARDS

This activity supports content standards in Health and Physical Education (see pages 9–14 for details).

MATERIALS NEEDED

• soft ball (tennis, softball, Nerf)

• five-gallon tub (available at do-it-yourself hardware stores)

• 1 coin

Getting Ready

Organize a space large enough to accommodate two teams in separate lines, either sitting on the floor or standing opposite one another. Place the bucket and ball beside each other at one end of the space between the last two people in the two lines. Determine how you will divide the large group into two smaller teams of equal number.

Activity

Divide the group into two equal teams. If you have an odd number of kids, have one serve as the coin toss "referee."

Arrange the teams into two lines (one line = one team), standing or sitting on the floor facing each other. Designate which end of the lines will be the starting point. If one of the group members is serving as the coin toss referee, have that person stand

103

at the head of the lines between the first two players; otherwise position yourself there.

Explain that the two teams are going to race each other by passing a hand squeeze down their lines. After the last person in the line gets the squeeze, he or she will pick up the ball and toss it into the bucket. The first team to grab the ball and toss it into the bucket wins the round. The winning team gets to rotate its players down one, with the last player going to the front. The first team to rotate every player through the entire line wins.

The catch is, there is no talking allowed, and all players except for the two people at the beginning of the lines have to keep their eyes closed during the entire race. Once the squeeze passes through a player's hands, that player can open his or her eyes, too—but there still should be no talking.

You or your coin-toss referee will silently start the activity by tossing a coin while the starting team members watch carefully to see if the coin lands on heads or tails. If it lands on tails, they are to do nothing. If it lands on heads, they will say nothing but will squeeze the hand of the person next to them, who will squeeze the hand of the person next to them with their other hand, and so on. When the squeeze reaches the end of the line, the last person must grab the ball and toss it in the bucket.

Answer any questions before starting. Once the activity is completed, acknowledge the teamwork and success of both groups, celebrate the winning team, and bring the group together to discuss.

Talk About It

Using terms your students will understand, ask questions like the following to help explore the leadership learning:

- How well do you feel your group worked together?

- Since you couldn't talk to one another, what type of communication skills did you use to accomplish this goal?

- How hard was it to remain patient and quiet and keep your eyes closed throughout the process?

- Were you ever in doubt that the squeeze was passed to you? If so, what did you do to make sure?

- Which role did you like the most? Which did you like the least? Explain.

- Did anyone emerge as a leader? Was it necessary for your team to have a leader for this activity? Why or why not?

- How did your team react when you lost a round?

- What did you do as a team to stay focused and on task?

- Can you relate this activity to any real-life team situations you've been in or expect to be in?

LEADERSHIP
Improv

With opportunities for numerous variations, "improv" (improvisation) lets kids be silly and have fun while gaining confidence performing or speaking in front of others. Like a game of charades, each child creates a card that others will receive randomly and then act out.

Time: 15–30 minutes (depending on group size and number of performers)

Age: Grades 3–6

Group Size: No limit

LEADERSHIP LEARNING CONCEPTS

- Public Speaking
- Creative Thinking

SUPPORTING STANDARDS

This activity supports content standards in ELA—Speaking and Listening, and ELA—Language (see pages 9–14 for details).

MATERIALS NEEDED

- index cards or blank scraps of paper
- writing utensils

Getting Ready

This activity requires no additional preparation unless you are conducting any of the Variations.

Activity

Invite kids to sit where they can see everyone in the group. This can be done at desks or tables, or you may want to have kids sit in a circle. Pass out one slip of paper and writing utensil to every child. Ask each person to write an action or activity on the piece of paper (such as bark like a dog, play basketball, march in a parade, or lead a cheer). When everyone is done, ask students to fold over the paper two times so no one can see what's written on the sheet.

Ask the group to start passing the papers around the circle in the same direction simultaneously and one spot at a time. Say "stop" after a few seconds (or, if you prefer, play music and turn it off when you want them to stop, as you would in a game of musical chairs). When asked to stop, each person holds onto the folded paper in his or her hand. Have one student unfold his or her card (everyone else should keep the paper folded) and do the action described on the piece of paper. The audience can cheer and encourage, and ultimately, guess what action the person is demonstrating. The child whose card it is should remain quiet and not shout out the answer.

Talk About It

Squeeze out the last giggles and calm down the group before asking questions like the following, using terms your students will understand, to help explore the leadership learning:

- When you wrote your action on the paper, did you think someone might have to perform it? If so, did you try to pick an action that was silly or might be embarrassing to someone?

- How do you feel when you have to talk or act in front of others?

- Is this feeling different if you are your group's leader and you have to talk in front of others on behalf of your group?

- What can you do to be comfortable doing new things in front of a group?

- What are some real-life examples of when you had to speak or do something in front of others? How did you feel while you were doing it? How did you feel afterward?

- What skills and behaviors are important for you to be a successful public speaker?

- What are some things you can do to get practice in public speaking? (If kids don't have many ideas, you might suggest getting involved in student council, standing in class when giving an answer, volunteering to be a group spokesperson when working on a project, speaking up on your sports team, and volunteering at a senior center in order to interact with people you don't know.)

Variations

1. Prior to conducting the session, prepare cards with diverse, everyday leadership actions you want kids to demonstrate. For example, "person conducting an orchestra," "doing a speech in front of your class," or "getting ready to run a race."

2. Prior to conducting the session, prepare cards with a variety of leadership words. Pass out the cards and ask kids to prepare a short speech (30 seconds to a minute) about what that word means to them. Encourage them to use real-life examples, if they can.

3. When each person performs, tell the audience they cannot laugh. If they laugh they're out; the process continues until only two people (the winners) are left.

4. On an index card, have each child draw or write the name of a famous leader or role model. Collect the cards and shuffle them. Have each person draw a card without letting others see what name is on the card. When each person's turn comes up, allow the student 30 seconds to a minute to act out that person, while the audience guesses who it is. Depending on the age and maturity of kids in the group, you may wish to prepare the leader cards ahead of time, as some kids may think of celebrities rather than leaders.

SESSION · SESSION · SESSION · SESSION ·

26

HOUSE
of Cards

This activity is divided into two parts. During the first part, small groups work independently to build the largest house of cards possible in a limited amount of time, without being able to talk with their own (or other) team members. Though unstated, the implication is that the groups are competing against one another. The second part requires the small groups to connect their different houses together within the same parameters.

Time: 45 minutes

Age: Grades 3–6

Group Size: Unlimited number of small groups of 4–6 members

Note: Brick Houses on page 94 is an alternate version designed for grades K–2.

LEADERSHIP LEARNING CONCEPTS

- Teamwork
- Problem Solving
- Communication
- Creative Thinking

SUPPORTING STANDARDS

This activity supports content standards in Math, and Health and Physical Education (see pages 9–14 for details).

MATERIALS NEEDED

- large supply (1,000 or more) of 3" x 5" index cards, library cards, or playing cards (about 20 decks); the more teams you have, the more cards you need

- a small plastic container—shoebox size or smaller, with a lid and handle, widely available at discount retailers—is a convenient way to store the cards

- ample floor or tabletop space for all teams to work on creating three-dimensional houses of cards, with room for individual houses to be connected to one another

Getting Ready

Depending on the space you use to conduct this activity, move any tables, chairs, or desks out of the way or together to create an open flat area for movement and building (either on the floor or on a flat surface). Determine the method you'll use to divide the larger group into smaller teams so participants are not selecting their own teammates. Place the cards (in a pile or in a small plastic container) in a central location where all teams have easy access while building. The more teams you have, the more cards you need.

Activity Part 1

Divide the larger group into smaller groups of four to five members each. Assign each team its own spot in the room, within reasonable proximity of one another in order to facilitate the second part of the activity. Explain the activity like this:

> In your small teams, you are to create a three-dimensional house of cards from the ground up. You will have 10 minutes to create your houses using only the cards. You may not use table legs, chairs, books, tape, paper clips, or any other items to support your houses, nor may you bend or tear any of the cards. There are two other rules. First, you cannot communicate verbally with each other to accomplish your goal—this means no talking, grunting, humming, or making other mouth sounds. Second, you cannot draw or illustrate any of your ideas. You have only 10 minutes to finish the house; if it falls any time during those 10 minutes, start over. Everyone in your group has to be happy with the final structure.

Take care not to set it up as a competition between the teams; this tends to naturally occur and can be addressed in discussion. As teams start building, watch to make sure groups keep their houses freestanding, with no support from other objects or items. Let them know when they have two to three minutes left. After 10 minutes, call time and have teams step away from their structures.

Talk About It

Using terms your students will understand, ask questions like the following to help explore the leadership learning:

- Did you achieve your goal? If so, was it hard? If not, what held you back?

- How did it feel to try to accomplish this goal without talking?

- How did you communicate?

- How did you know when everyone in your group was happy and you'd achieved your goal?

- How did your group deal with frustration? For example, if your house fell down, how did your group react and get going again?

- Did you feel like you were competing against the other group(s)? Why or why not?

Activity Part 2

After discussion, inform the separate teams that they will use more cards and work together to connect all of the structures together. The no-talking rule still applies, as do all the other rules. The connecting structure must also be three-dimensional (not a flat path, for example), with no other support systems. Again, the connection is not complete until everyone in the group is satisfied. Allow 10 to 15 minutes for teams to work together to accomplish this. Call time, celebrate completion, and discuss.

Talk About It

Using terms your students will understand, ask questions like the following to help explore the leadership learning:

- Did you achieve your goal? If so, was it hard? If not, what held you back?

- What was it like to work with the entire group to accomplish a goal? How was it different from working with your small group?

- How did the attitude of competition change when working on the goal this time?

- How did your group communicate this time?

- How did your group know when everyone was happy and had achieved its goal?

- How would this activity have been different if you could talk?

- Did anyone act like a leader during this activity? If so, how did the person become the leader? Did having a leader help you achieve the goal? Explain.

- Was this like real life in any way? How?

Extension

Consider challenging kids to observe how people (themselves included) use nonverbal skills and rely on other strategies for communicating with others. If you ask them to do this, take 5 to 10 minutes the next time the group gets together to have them share what they observed.

SESSION · SESSION · SESSION · SESSION

27

PUZZLE

Kids work in pairs, one person guiding the other, putting together a set of geometric shapes to create a puzzle. The pairs attempt the task in three different ways, twice with limitations on how they communicate, and finally with as much back-and-forth conversation as necessary.

Time: 25–35 minutes

Age: Grades 3–6

Group Size: No limit, although even numbers work best

LEADERSHIP LEARNING CONCEPTS

• Communication

• Problem Solving

• Teamwork

• Group Dynamics

SUPPORTING STANDARDS

This activity supports content standards in ELA—Speaking and Listening, and Math (see pages 9–14 for details).

MATERIALS NEEDED

• card stock or other stiff paper

• scissors

• resealable plastic sandwich bags, one for each pair of kids

• folder or envelope to hold 8½" x 11" paper

• ample floor space for partners to work independently of other paired teams

• "Puzzle Key" handout (page 113)

• see Variations for other materials you may need, if necessary

Getting Ready

On card stock or other stiff paper, make one copy of the "Puzzle Key" handout for each pair of kids. For each handout, cut out the puzzle pieces along the lines and place the pieces in a resealable plastic bag. Seal the bag.

On regular paper, make one copy of the "Puzzle Key" for each pair of kids. This is the master design for the puzzle, so don't cut up these copies; place them in a folder where the completed design cannot be seen. Organize the room so that there is ample space on the floor where kids can sit back-to-back in pairs.

Activity

This activity is designed with three stages. In the first stage, one partner tries to correctly assemble a puzzle after receiving instructions from the other partner but without being able to ask questions. In the second stage, the person attempts the same task, but this time is able to ask yes-and-no questions. In the third and final attempt, the two partners are able to talk freely.

Partner up all of the kids. You can choose to do this using a neutral format (such as counting off by twos) or allow kids to select their own partner. Have each pair identify who will be partner "A" and who will be partner "B." They will maintain these roles throughout the activity. Once they have identified their roles, have them sit on the floor, back-to-back, each unable to see what the other is doing. Explain the activity by saying:

> **I will give each team a jumbled set of puzzle shapes. "A" partners, you are going to receive a copy of the shapes put into an organized geometric pattern—this is the puzzle answer key. Keep this out of the view of partner "B." "B" partners, you will receive the shapes in a plastic bag. Staying exactly where you are, with your backs to each other, partner "A" will give partner "B" instructions for putting the puzzle together.**

> **Once the activity begins, you'll get three tries to finish the puzzle. Each try has different rules. The goal in all three attempts is for "A" partners to communicate to "B" partners what they need to know to put the puzzle together as a match to the puzzle key. Wait until I say to start each try.**

Pass out the puzzle keys to all "A" partners and the bags of geometric shapes to all "B" partners. Then continue:

> **Here are the rules for your first try. Partner "A" will explain to partner "B" how to put the puzzle together. For this first attempt, only partner "A" can speak. Partner "B" cannot speak or ask questions. You have five minutes.**

Walk around the room making sure that "B" partners remain quiet and cannot see the answer keys held by any "A" partners. (If teams are sitting close together, you might also want to make sure that none of the "B" partners can see a puzzle key that an "A" partner on a different team is holding.) Call time at five minutes, regardless of whether teams have finished their puzzles. Then instruct the group for the second attempt by saying:

> **It's time to try again. Partner "B," if you don't think you solved the puzzle the first time, you'll have another chance now. If you do think you solved it, partner "A" will rotate (turn) the answer key so the puzzle design is different this time. Partner "A" will again tell you how to put the puzzle together. This time, you can ask partner "A" questions that can be answered with "yes" or "no" only. Again, you have five minutes.**

Walk around the room making sure that partners are asking and answering only yes-and-no questions. Call time at five minutes, regardless of whether teams have finished their puzzles. Then instruct the group for the final attempt by saying:

> **Once again, if you think partner "B" solved the puzzle, partner "A" should rotate the key so the puzzle design is different from both earlier tries. Partner "A," you're still trying to help partner "B" solve the puzzle. Although neither partner can see what the other is doing, you can both talk freely through this attempt. You have five minutes.**

This attempt is likely to go quickly and smoothly; still, call time at five minutes regardless of whether teams have finished their puzzles. Allow partners to look together at the key and the final result.

Talk About It

Ask for volunteers to talk about what it was like to be partner "A" and partner "B" in each of the three different phases of the activity. Then, using terms your students will understand, ask questions like the following to help explore the leadership learning:

- Did you like being in your role? If not, what would you change? If you have a team job to do in real life, which role would you prefer to be in? Explain.

- Describe how you and your partner communicated during each of the different attempts.

- What happens in a group when one person has more information than others? How can members of a group deal with this type of situation?

- Can you think of some real-life situations where you tried solving a problem but didn't have all the "pieces"—that is, all the information—you needed? How would things have been different if you'd had more information or if others had communicated more clearly while you tried to solve the problem?

- What happens when one person in your group has a certain goal in mind but can't clearly communicate it to the group?

- What do you think people can do to become better communicators? (Suggest things such as attitude, tone of voice, loudness and softness of voice, mumbling, organizing their thoughts ahead of time, and thinking before speaking.) **Note:** You may want to have kids respond to this question in a separate brainstorm session.

Variations

1. Rather than use an answer key, have "A" partners create their own designs using puzzle pieces from their bag, and then have "B" partners duplicate it. After each attempt, allow partner "A" to show partner "B" his or her design and allow them to compare puzzles. "A" partners will need to put the puzzle together in a different way for each attempt. Otherwise the activity and discussion proceed in the same way, with no questions for the first attempt, yes-and-no questions for the second, and free conversation for the third, followed by the "Talk About It" discussion. You will need two bags of puzzle pieces per set of partners, rather than one "Puzzle Key" and one baggie of pieces.

2. Create a large-scale version of the geometric shapes using a 4' x 8' sheet of particle board (widely available at do-it-yourself building stores). Sketch the geometric shapes (in larger format) on the particle board (or draw a traditional "jigsaw" puzzle design) and, using a circular saw, cut them out. Plan on dividing a large group into smaller teams of five to six kids. Make as many sets of the large puzzle as necessary for the number of small teams you'll have. Small teams compete with one another to put together the puzzle, with one person holding the puzzle key and communicating without showing the design to the rest of the group. If you wish, impose the same restrictions as described in the original activity. Discuss what made each team successful, how each team worked together to problem solve, communication styles used, and so on.

3. Select two or three kids to serve as leaders. Arrange everyone else in a circle on the floor with blindfolds on. Dump a large piece children's jigsaw puzzle (20 to 30 pieces) on the floor in the middle of the circle. The leaders are tasked with communicating with the group to put together the puzzle. The leaders may not touch the puzzle pieces and the blindfolded team members may not speak.

Extension

Repeat the original activity (or any variation) at a different time, using a more complex puzzle or having kids work together on a real, larger puzzle; let the communication and problem solving be free flowing. Refer back to the original Puzzle activity and the differences in solving puzzles when communication and teamwork roadblocks are imposed.

PUZZLE Key

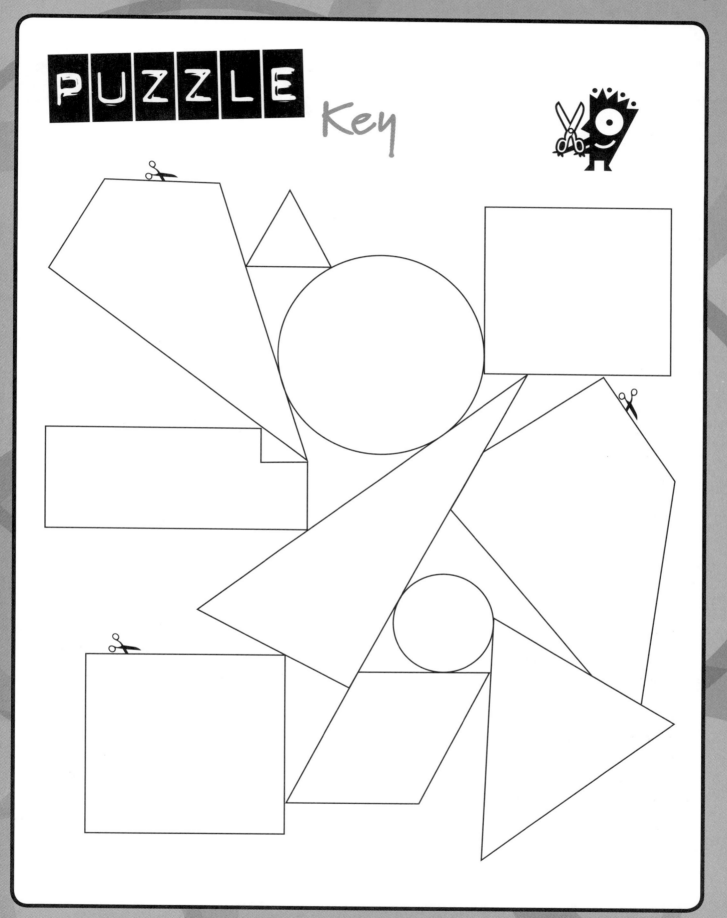

SESSION · SESSION · SESSION · SESSION ·

28

SNOWFLAKE

Through following directions for creating a simple paper snowflake, kids learn how everyone can interpret the same information differently, reinforcing the importance of clear communication and active listening.

Time: 20 minutes

Age: Grades 3–6

Group Size: No limit

LEADERSHIP LEARNING CONCEPTS

- Communication
- Active Listening

SUPPORTING STANDARDS

This activity supports content standards in ELA—Speaking and Listening and ELA—Writing (Extension) (see pages 9–14 for details).

MATERIALS NEEDED

- sheets of white 8½" x 11" paper

Activity

Pass out a piece of paper to each child.

Explain to kids that you want them to follow the directions you are about to give without asking questions and without paying attention to or working with others in the group. Then give the following directions quickly, without clarifying exactly what you mean, pausing only briefly between steps.

1. Fold the paper in half and tear off the top corner.

2. Fold it in half again and tear off the top corner.

3. Fold it in half again and tear off the left corner.

4. Rotate the paper to the right three times and tear off the bottom corner.

5. Fold it in half again and tear off a middle piece.

Instruct the group to unfold their papers and compare their snowflakes with those around them. Individual snowflakes may or may not match others.

Talk About It

Encourage comments about the similarities and differences among the snowflakes. Then, using terms your students will understand, ask questions like the following to help explore the leadership learning:

- How well do you think you listened to the instructions?

- Why do you think that even though everyone received the same directions, your snowflakes don't all look the same?

- What do you think would have changed if you'd been able to ask questions?

- Have you ever told someone one thing only to have the person hear and do something different? What happened, and how did you deal with it?

- If you are the leader of a team or group, what can you do to make sure others clearly understand you?

- What do you need to do differently (as a communicator) if others are seeing things differently than you intended?

Extension

Conduct the activity with kids attempting to get everyone to make an identical snowflake by presenting very specific directions to their classmates. Prior to leading the group, have students complete an assignment that involves writing out their directions. Discuss how differently the activity went when the directions were clearly spelled out. You may also choose to allow students to ask questions while their classmates are instructing.

SESSION · SESSION · SESSION · SESSION

29

BACK/FEEDBACK

This activity gives kids an opportunity to offer feedback and positive comments to others in a low-risk way. Pieces of construction paper are taped to participants' backs and everyone writes brief notes on each other's sheets. Build in time at the end for kids to read people's comments privately and acknowledge one another if desired.

Time: 15–25 minutes (depending on group size)

Age: Grades 3–6

Group Size: No limit

Note: Word List Feedback on page 92 is an alternate version of this activity designed for grades K–2.

LEADERSHIP LEARNING CONCEPTS

- Appreciating Others
- Feedback

SUPPORTING STANDARDS

This activity supports content standards in ELA—Writing and ELA—Language (see pages 9–14 for details).

MATERIALS NEEDED

- sturdy drawing paper or construction paper
- markers that won't puncture or bleed through the paper, one or more for each participant
- masking tape
- dry-erase board or interactive whiteboard
- Optional: "Sample Personality Adjective List"
- Optional: chart paper (for Variation)

Getting Ready

On the dry-erase board or interactive whiteboard, write a list of positive and encouraging adjectives that describe people. You can use the "Sample Personality Adjective List" on page 118 for ideas. Select words familiar to your group. If you include

more challenging words, take time with your group to explore definitions and usage in context.

Activity

Ask kids to select a piece of paper and one or more markers and write their names at the top of their papers. With the help of other group members, have participants tape the sheet of paper to their backs. Once everyone is prepared, begin the activity by saying:

> **The paper on your back is a place for your fellow group members to write a note of thanks, mention something they've learned from you, or offer other appreciative words about what you've brought to the group. You will do the same on their papers. You can move around as you wish in order to write on everyone's back. Please keep your messages positive and honest; avoid jokes or insider comments. You don't have to write a lot, but you want your messages to be meaningful and memorable. If you are comfortable doing so, sign your name so people know who wrote the note. Write at least one thing on every person's paper.**

If you have a large group, you can assure that no one is left out by dividing the group into two lines facing one another. Have line "A" be the signers first, then line "B." Once they finish, move each line one person to the right until everyone has written on one another's sheet. Ask participants to leave the papers on their backs until everyone has written on each person's sheet. Bring the group together to remove their sheets at the same time. You may choose to have group members find private space or sit in a circle while they read their messages.

Talk About It

If this activity is being used as a closure activity (at the end of a school year or specific leadership experience), you may want to reserve 5 to 10 minutes for kids to share what it meant to be part of the group or to comment on what people wrote. Pay attention to include everyone in the group and make sure each member is recognized during the final discussion.

Consider these additional prompts:

- Does anyone want to acknowledge specific comments someone else wrote to you?

- Overall, what would you say about your experience as part of this group?

Variations

1. Some kids may be more comfortable writing comments on larger sheets of paper and a more stable surface. In this case, have kids tape individual sheets of chart paper to the wall, writing their name large enough at the top so others can easily read it. Then have participants move from sheet to sheet writing messages of support and appreciation. Make sure that everyone writes on everyone else's sheet and that students don't read their own sheets until the entire rotation is complete. **Note:** This is a higher risk version of the activity because everyone can clearly see and read what others wrote.

2. If you have access to a laminating machine, you may offer to laminate the Back/Feedback papers prior to everyone taking them home. You can also make reduced copies of the sheets so kids can use them as bookmarks for a regular reminder of what others appreciate about them.

Sample PERSONALITY Adjective List

adaptable	diplomatic	independent	practical
adventurous	dynamic	intellectual	quiet
agreeable	easygoing	intelligent	rational
ambitious	empathetic	intuitive	reliable
amusing	energetic	inventive	reserved
athletic	enthusiastic	kind	resourceful
brave	exceptional	logical	responsible
bright	fair-minded	loving	self-confident
calm	faithful	loyal	self-disciplined
caring	fearless	modest	sensible
cautious	friendly	neat	sensitive
charming	funny	nice	shy
compassionate	generous	optimistic	sincere
conscientious	gentle	outgoing	smart
considerate	good	passionate	straightforward
courageous	hardworking	patient	thoughtful
courteous	helpful	persistent	tough
creative	honest	philosophical	understanding
decisive	humble	pioneering	versatile
determined	humorous	polite	warmhearted
diligent	imaginative	powerful	witty

TEAMBUILDING
and Working with Others

Understanding what it means to be part of a team starts to become a familiar concept to kids once they enter school. They begin to grasp the difference between being part of a "group," that may or may not share things in common, to being part of a "team," where teamwork and pride are important. The activities in this section focus on building relationships among kids in groups, as they strive to achieve common goals. They turn into a team and learn what's necessary for that team to succeed together. Teambuilding activities promote cooperation and communication. They enrich classroom culture by teaching firsthand what it means to say, *the sum is greater than its parts!*

BIRTHDAY
Line Up

Without speaking or using any props, kids work together to organize their group in order by birthday. This activity requires resourceful communication skills, teamwork, and trust.

Time: 15–20 minutes (depending on group size)

Age: Grades K–6

Group Size: No limit

Note: The Variation is better suited for grades 3–6.

LEADERSHIP LEARNING CONCEPTS

- Teamwork
- Resourcefulness

SUPPORTING STANDARDS

This activity supports content standards in Math, and Health and Physical Education (see pages 9–14 for details).

MATERIALS NEEDED

- Optional: index cards (Variation)
- Optional: blindfolds (Variation)

Getting Ready

Move any chairs, tables, or desks out of the way so the group has a safe, open space in which to move around.

Activity

Explain to the students that they have one goal to achieve: to line themselves up in order of their birthdays. Before they begin, offer a more specific explanation:

In this game, your goal is to line yourselves up in order of birthdays, by month and day (year doesn't matter). It's up to you as a group to make sure everyone agrees which end of the line marks January and December, and when everyone in between is in the correct order. The catch is, you're going to do this without speaking with one another. You also can't use any other things around the room, such as a calendar, bulletin board, paper, or pen. You may, of course, use your body. Any questions?

Answer any questions, unless someone starts asking you about other people's birthdays! Remind them that there are many different ways to get information across to others without talking. You can also correlate this activity to sequencing numbers in math. If there are no questions, tell the group to start.

When the group agrees they've got the line correct, ask each person to state his or her birthday, beginning with the end of the line they've chosen to be January. There are many ways for groups to complete this task, for example, holding up various combinations of fingers, writing on one another's palms, or stomping on the floor in different patterns to represent month, then day.

Talk About It

Using terms your students will understand, ask questions like the following to help explore the leadership learning:

- How did your group accomplish the goal?

- Who was the first to figure out a way to line up? Did you find a pattern or way to communicate? Describe the method you used.

- Did someone become the leader? How and why? If not, do you think you needed one? Why or why not?

- What did you learn about how you usually communicate with others?

Variation

Older kids may easily accomplish the activity as described. If that's the case, consider adding this more complex variation (or use it in place of the original). Get a number of index cards equal to the number of kids in your group and write a number on each card from 1 to _____ (the total number of kids in the group). Pass one card randomly to each person, asking him or her not to share the number with others. Have the group form a circle. Have everyone close their eyes and keep them closed for the rest of the activity (or if you prefer, use blindfolds). Have kids hold hands with the person next to them, before stepping back until everyone's arms are fully extended. Have them drop hands and in silence, organize the line into order by numbers. Afterward, discuss the experience by including these questions with the previous ones:

- What was it like to be blindfolded (or keep your eyes closed)?

- Did you trust the other people around you? Why or why not?

- Can you think of any real-life situations where you had to trust other team members or the leader, even if you couldn't see how they were contributing to your group's goals?

SESSION · SESSION · SESSION · SESSION

31

PRETZEL
Pass

The object of the activity is for each team to pass a pretzel from the front of their line to the last person in the line, using only straws in their mouths. The fastest team wins. While simple in concept, this activity can be challenging for students. If you prefer, you can do this as a timed exercise with the whole group or among several small teams instead of between two teams as described.

Time: 15 minutes

Age: Grades 3–6

Group Size: No limit

Note: With second-grade students, their less developed eye-hand dexterity may mean you'll need to allot more than 15 minutes for this activity.

LEADERSHIP LEARNING CONCEPTS

- Creative Thinking
- Goal Setting
- Patience

SUPPORTING STANDARDS

This activity supports content standards in Health and Physical Education (see pages 9–14 for details).

MATERIALS NEEDED

- small pretzels (circles or traditional shape, not sticks)
- sturdy drinking straws, one for each participant

Activity

Divide the large group into teams of 8 to 15 each, then partner two teams to compete against one another. If you have a small group, this activity still works with teams of four to five. Arrange each pair of teams into two equal lines facing each other. Pass out a straw to each participant. Pass out one pretzel to the person at the head of each line. Explain the activity like this:

The object of this activity is for each team to pass the pretzel from the front of your line to the last person in your line, using only the straw in your

mouths. For the first round, you can use your hands to guide your own straw, but you can't talk with others on your team. After doing it this way, you're going to do it again, with different rules.

If necessary, invite two volunteers to demonstrate using the straw in their mouths to pass the pretzel before beginning the first round. During the first round, allow no time for teams to strategize, nor any verbal communication from the point you say "go." Allow team members to use their hands to control the direction of their own straw but not another person's straw.

After completing the first round, have the teams compete without using hands or other body parts to guide their straws. For this round, however, provide three to five minutes for the teams to strategize before saying "go." Also explain that teams can communicate openly with each other the entire time they're passing the pretzel from straw to straw.

In both rounds, if the pretzel falls to the ground at any time, the team must start over. The first team to get their pretzel to the end wins.

Talk About It

Collect the straws and pretzels to minimize distractions. Using terms your students will understand, ask questions like the following to help explore the leadership learning:

- The idea of this game was pretty easy. How was it to actually play?

- How did your group work together the first time, when you didn't get a chance to make a plan?

- How did things change when you were able to make a plan and communicate with each other?

- How did your group overcome any challenges that came up during the activity?

- What real-life situations does this activity make you think of?

GROUP
Juggling

This activity encourages groups to work together to set and achieve team goals. Everyone in the group plays an important role in achieving the goal. Team members must pay attention to both verbal and nonverbal (eye contact or signals) communication and feedback in order to succeed.

Time: 20–30 minutes

Age: Grades 3–6

Group Size: No limit

LEADERSHIP LEARNING CONCEPTS

- Communication
- Goal Setting
- Teamwork

SUPPORTING STANDARDS

This activity supports content standards in ELA—Speaking and Listening, Math, and Health and Physical Education (see pages 9–14 for details).

MATERIALS NEEDED

- soft balls, stuffed animals, or other items of some weight (softball size or smaller), as many (or more) as there are kids in the group
- five-gallon empty plastic paint tub or other large plastic bucket with a top
- digital stopwatch or wristwatch with timer

Getting Ready

Collect the soft items and store them in the bucket. Move any tables, desks, and chairs to the sides to create a large open area (or ask kids to assist before starting the session).

Activity

Organize the group into a circle (standing or sitting). If you have a large group, you may divide them into two or three smaller circles to increase engagement. Describe the activity like this:

I am going to hand a ball (or other item) to one of you to be the Starter. The Starter will toss it to someone in the circle who is not directly next to him or her. The next person will do the same, tossing it to someone who hasn't yet received the ball, and so on, until everyone has tossed and received the ball once. The last person will toss the ball back to the Starter. Pay attention because, as you do this, you are creating a pattern that you'll have to repeat later!

There are a couple of rules for when you pass the ball to each other. First, the ball must remain in the air. If you bounce it toward a person or drop it, the group has to start over. Also, to make sure others are paying attention to you, say the name of the person you're throwing to *before* you toss the ball.

Give the ball to a Starter and ask that student to begin. Take note of the pattern the group uses so you can check it on future rounds. When they finish, have them do it again in the same pattern. For the third round, time the group using the stopwatch. After telling the group how fast they were, give them a goal to beat that time or ask them to set a goal for how fast they think they can do their pattern. Have them repeat the pattern until they beat the time or decide they're satisfied with their time.

Now have them complete the pattern using more balls. Let the group choose how many more so that they are still in control of their team goal. The additional balls are to be passed around the pattern one at a time, rather than all at the same time. Once the group has completed the pattern a few times with the additional balls, time them again and then challenge them to beat that time. Encourage the group to stop, strategize, and start, as they desire. To increase the challenge, add even more balls.

Keep timing with the stopwatch to see how well the group can do before the game becomes too chaotic.

Talk About It

Collect the balls or other items when done to minimize distractions. Using terms your students will understand, ask questions like the following to help explore the leadership learning:

- What are some things you did that helped you succeed?

- How did you communicate with each other? Think about what you said as well as any looks, movements, sounds, or other ways you communicated.

- How well do you think you communicated—as individuals and as members of the group?

- Do you think the group would have been faster if you'd had a leader directing you? Why or why not?

- When you started getting timed, did your attitude change (as an individual or as a group)? For example, did you feel nervous, excited, determined, or competitive?

- How well do you think your team worked together?

- Can you relate this activity to any real-life team situations you've been in or expect to be in?

SESSION 33

SPAGHETTI TRAIN
Obstacle Course

Using uncooked (raw) spaghetti noodles to link individual group members, the team must move as quickly as possible through an obstacle course set up around the room, without letting go or breaking the noodles.

Time: 30 minutes (depending on group size, number of groups, and number of obstacles)

Age: Grades 3–6

Group Size: Small groups of 8–12 work best

Note: Multiple teams can go through the same obstacle course, competing with one another, or you can set up a different obstacle course and have teams go through each of them, setting goals and competing only with the goals they set for their individual team.

LEADERSHIP LEARNING CONCEPTS

- Teamwork
- Goal Setting
- Communication
- Leadership Basics

SUPPORTING STANDARDS

This activity supports content standards in ELA—Speaking and Listening, and Health and Physical Education (see pages 9–14 for details).

MATERIALS NEEDED

- large box of raw, unbroken spaghetti noodles
- mats, hula hoops, chairs, tables, tunnels, and other materials to make a simple obstacle course (or if available, use an outdoor space or playground)
- timer or stopwatch

Getting Ready

Using the materials listed or other obstacles, create a reasonable obstacle course for teams to pass through. Keep in mind the height and physical abilities of all kids in the group so as to avoid expecting teams to climb over mats or other items that are too high, or squeeze through areas that are too small.

This activity can be conducted outside. If setting up the course outside, use playground equipment or other outdoor obstacles, such as trees, rocks, and benches as obstacles.

Activity

Allow kids to look at and get excited about doing the obstacle course laid out before them. Explain that the group is going to try getting through the obstacle course as quickly as possible. In addition, they want to avoid getting any penalties by breaking (literally!) the one rule. The one rule: They have to get through the course while connected together by pieces of raw spaghetti held between team members, reaching their destination without letting go of or breaking any of the noodles. If a noodle breaks, the entire team has to stop, remain in their spots, and wait for the leader to give them a new unbroken noodle. Once the leader has returned to the front of the line, the group may start the course again. Add five seconds to the team's time for each noodle that breaks.

After explaining the activity, allow two to three minutes for the group to select a leader. Have the leader pass out a spaghetti noodle to each group member. Provide the leader with 20 extra noodles to replace any that break during the activity. Each person will hold one end of the noodle while the person ahead of him or her holds the other.

Ask the leader to tell you when his or her team is ready to go. At that point, say "go" and time the team as it walks the course. Record the time and keep track of how many broken noodles are replaced. If more than one team is completing the course, have each team take its turn before moving on to the next section.

Have the students discuss how they will try to beat their time for the next round. You might suggest deciding between going as fast as possible, with the possibility of broken noodles (and added penalty seconds); or going slower, with fewer broken noodles.

If time allows, the group can do the course additional times to try to set new records. If more than one team is completing the course and competing against the others, state the final score and declare a winner. Celebrate achievements and discuss the experience after completing the second (or third) pass through.

Talk About It

Using terms your students will understand, ask questions like the following to help explore the leadership learning:

- How did your group select the leader? Did you feel confident with your decision throughout the entire activity? Why or why not?

- Other than being first in line, how did your leader act as a leader?

- Leader: Do you think you did more for your group than walk first in line? Explain. Also, how did it feel to be the leader?

- What was it like to be a follower in this activity?

- Was there ever a time when someone else wanted to become the leader? How about a time the leader wanted to trade roles with a follower?

- Are you more of a follower or leader in your everyday life? Explain.

- How important is the role of a good follower? Are there any situations where it's better to be a follower than a leader? Explain.

- How did you feel while doing the obstacle course? (Ask several team members and compare answers. What similarities and differences do the kids notice in responses?)

- How did you feel (or what was your reaction) when a noodle broke? (Ask several team members and compare answers. What similarities and differences do the kids notice in responses?)

- What was hard about this activity? What was easy about it?

- Are there any things you wish your group had done differently? If so, what and why?

- How can you apply this activity to real life?

PIPELINE

With each team member holding one segment of plastic (PVC) pipe, individuals work together to transfer a golf ball from one tube to another to reach a target. The path they follow can be marked with tape on the floor (like a winding "road"), or the group can determine a path that gets them from the starting line across the finishing line (a designated target located at a distance in the room).

Time: 20–30 minutes (depending on group size)

Age: Grades 3–6

Group Size: No limit

LEADERSHIP LEARNING CONCEPTS

- Teamwork
- Creative Thinking
- Resourcefulness
- Goal Setting

SUPPORTING STANDARDS

This activity supports content standards in ELA—Speaking and Listening, Math, and Health and Physical Education (see pages 9–14 for details).

MATERIALS NEEDED

- 12" segments of 2"-diameter PVC pipe, one segment for every child in the group (available at do-it-yourself hardware stores; have the store cut the PVC for you). If you wish to increase the activity challenge, cut the PVC into lengths varying from 10" to 24"
- 1 or more golf balls
- 2 gallon bucket, shoe box, or other sturdy container
- masking or blue painter's tape
- Optional: obstacles such as milk crates, low or high stools (easy to get around), hula hoops to step through or around, and foam "noodles" or balance beams to lay across the path (Variation)
- Optional: timer or stopwatch (Variation)
- Optional: instead of PVC pipe and golf balls, you can use empty paper towel tubes and small bouncy balls or marbles

Getting Ready

Purchase PVC tubing at a hardware store cut into 12" (one foot) segments (or other lengths as indicated in "Materials Needed"). Collect all other materials.

Organize the room so that kids have ample space to move around. Using the tape, mark a starting line and finish line, and place the bucket behind the finish line. If desired, lay tape in a line on the floor to create a path for kids to follow from start to finish. Otherwise, allow the students to get from the starting line to the finish line following the path that develops while the group moves with the pipes and ball(s).

Activity

Pass out a PVC section to each child, but hold onto the golf ball as you explain the activity. Explain that every kid in the group will hold a pipe segment, and the group will transfer a golf ball through all the segments from the starting line to the finish line following the path marked with tape (or along a path they create). The pipes and the golf ball may not touch the floor or any part of a team member or clothing. Also, the ball must go through everyone's tube before hitting the target. When the golf ball is in a student's tube, the student may not move his or her feet or hand off the tube to someone else. Other than that, the team may get the ball from the starting line to the finishing line any way they want.

Allow a few minutes for the group to make a plan, but don't allow them to practice passing the ball with their tubes.

When the group is ready, tell them to begin. If the ball drops on the floor while they are working toward the finish line, remind them that they must begin again.

Talk About It

Using terms your students will understand, ask questions like the following to help explore the leadership learning:

- Did someone on your team act as a leader as you completed the activity? If so, do you think that helped your team finish? Explain. Why do you think that person became the leader? If the person who became the leader is the same person who usually does, what can your group do to get other kids (or yourself) to step up?

- What plan or strategy did your team come up with to complete the course? Did the plan help? How could it have been better?

- Did everyone on the team get a chance to contribute to the plan if they wanted to?

- Was there ever a time during this activity where you felt like others weren't listening to you?

- What did you learn about trust and working with others during this activity?

- Give an example of how you can apply this activity to a real situation in your own life.

Variations

These variations increase the level of challenge involved in the original activity as well as increase the need for groups to deliberately strategize in order to succeed. Depending on your group, a few additional minutes may need to be allocated for activity completion.

1. Create an obstacle course through which the team must move in order to reach the target destination. Allow time for the group to strategize prior to beginning, but don't let them practice using the tubes and ball. For fourth, fifth, and sixth graders, this type of challenge adds an excellent element to keep them focused and working together, especially if you think they might easily accomplish the original activity.

2. Instead of laying out a path ahead of time, place the destination bucket in a particular location that requires the group to strategize the best (most efficient) path to reach it.

3. Have the group successfully accomplish the original activity without being timed. After they do, time the group as they do the course again, and then have them set a goal regarding how quickly they can make it through.

If doing any of the variations, consider these questions in addition to the previous ones:

- How difficult or easy was it for your team to get through the obstacle course?

- What got in your way? How did you make it through the obstacles before you?

- How well do you feel others on the team listened to your ideas? Explain.

- How did things change for your team as soon as you found out you'd be timed?

ISLAND
Statues

The team attempts to balance all together on a small, easy-to-make raised platform. For the first round, the team simply gets everyone safely to the "island." For subsequent attempts, the group is given progressively more difficult goals, from balancing on the platform for a certain length of time to creating more complicated "statue" designs that depend on everyone in the group.

Time: 20–30 minutes

Age: Grades 3–6

Group Size: 12–15; larger groups can be divided into multiple teams of 12–15 each

Note: See "Getting Ready" for building instructions to make a portable wooden platform. As an alternative to building a wooden platform, you can use 4" x 6" or 4" x 12" concrete paving blocks (enough to create an 18" x 18" or 24" x 24" raised area).

LEADERSHIP LEARNING CONCEPTS

- Teamwork
- Creative Thinking
- Patience

SUPPORTING STANDARDS

This activity supports content standards in Health and Physical Education, and Service Learning (see pages 9–14 for details).

MATERIALS NEEDED

- 8-foot 2" x 4" boards (if building the smaller platform, you need one; for the larger platform, you need two)
- plywood or MDF board (18" square or 24" square, depending on size of platform)
- masking tape
- timer or stopwatch

Getting Ready

Determine what size platform you want to build. For younger kids (who have smaller feet), an 18" x 18" platform easily fits 12 to 15 kids. If you want to fit a larger group size (or a group with older kids) onto a platform, build a 24" x 24" platform. This can be used with teens and adults as well. Modify your size based on the age and size of the kids in your group.

Cut the 2" x 4" into four 16" or 22" lengths, depending on the size of your desired platform. Lay them on their 2" edges so they nestle together into a square shape like this:

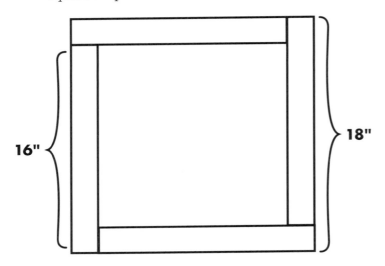

Nail the boards together in this shape to form the base of your platform. Lay the 18" x 18" or 24" x 24" piece of plywood or MDF board (dense particle board) on top of the base and nail it around the edges to secure to the base. Looking at the platform placed flat on the ground, it should look like this:

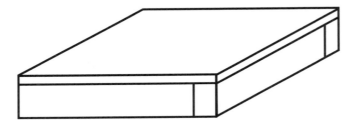

If using concrete paving blocks instead, organize them to create a similar 18" x 18" (or 24" x 24") square platform. Make sure the paving blocks are stable on the floor and that you have room for kids to move around the platform.

Place the platform in the center of the area you'll use for the activity. Put a square of masking tape all around the platform, two-to-four feet away from the platform (closer to the platform for younger and smaller kids, farther away for older and bigger kids).

If you don't want to build a reusable platform or use paving blocks, you can use small gym mats laid on top of one another or a low-raised cube mat that is no larger than 24" x 24" (smaller for younger kids), but be careful with this arrangement because mats can be slippery and tend to slip off one another.

Activity

To set the scene, create a storyline like the following:

Other than where we are standing on the shore (outside the area marked with tape), the only other safe spot in this room is your island (the platform). In between the shore and the island is a moat filled with alligators. Lucky for us, the alligators are sleeping, so the team can take its time getting everyone safely from the shore onto the island without stepping into or touching the alligators. There is no rule about leaning, reaching, or stretching over the moat.

Because you're dealing with sleepy gators, take your time coming up with a plan before trying to get each person, one by one, onto the platform. Once you have made it to the platform, you cannot step off to help or trade places with others. After your entire group is safely on board, all of you must remain still on the platform for 15 seconds to keep from waking the alligators. If anyone steps into the moat or falls off the island, they lose the use of the body part that landed in the water. This means they can't stand on that leg or foot, so the rest of the team may need to help them balance. If anyone falls off before the 15 seconds is up, the entire team starts again.

Remember, though, if anyone has lost the use of a leg or foot, your team will have to take this into consideration.

Answer any questions. When the group is ready, say "go." Pay attention to make sure people aren't stepping into the moat. Once the group makes it to the platform, time their frozen poses for 15 seconds. Celebrate the accomplishment before asking them to return from the platform to the shore. Then announce that the alligators have woken up and are beginning to inch toward the shore.

Uh, oh, the gators are awake. That means this time you all need to make it to the platform in a quick fashion, before they can eat you. But because these alligators appreciate art, they won't eat you if you're able to get the team onto the platform and get yourselves into a statue in the shape of your choice. You will then hold that shape for 15 seconds until the alligators sink back beneath the water. The same rule about losing body parts applies.

Answer any questions. When the group is ready, say "go." After they finish, celebrate the accomplishment. Ask the group if they have any goals they want to achieve on the platform, such as holding their statue longer, forming a different statue, and so on. Allow time for this, if desired.

Talk About It

Using terms your students will understand, ask questions like the following to help explore the leadership learning:

- How well did your team work together?
- What was the hardest part of this activity for your group?
- Did your team need a leader? If so, how did you choose one, or how did someone emerge as a leader?
- How well did you trust others on your team—to get all of you onto the platform and then to hold everyone there?
- Often the tallest person in the group and the smallest in the group have clear roles—the tallest can get to the platform first, the smallest can crouch down or is light and easy to hold. Knowing this, what can you do to uncover everyone's "gifts" and how these "gifts" contribute to a team's success?
- In what ways can you apply this activity to situations you've encountered in your daily lives?

Problem Solving and DECISION MAKING

Outside of math classes, most kids are unfamiliar with the phrase "problem-solving." Often when kids face problems with others, we urge them to turn to adults for help. The same is true about making decisions. For children, decision making frequently involves choosing between options given to them by adults. These decisions also aren't typically of great importance (blue shirt or green one? cheeseburger or chicken tenders?). When *real* decisions need making and *real* problems need solving, it's important that all kids feel prepared to take them on. This section presents problem solving and decision making simulations that actively engage kids in determining the outcome.

*Contains modifications for students transitioning to middle school

SESSION · SESSION · 36 · SESSION · SESSION

WOULD YOU
Rather?

Kids are presented with various "Would you rather?" questions relating to leadership and life and discuss their answers.

Time: 15–30 minutes (depending on number of questions asked and discussion)

Age: Grades K–6

Group Size: No limit

Note: This activity can also be used as a writing or discussion activity. Choose one or two options from the "Would You Rather Questions" handout and have students write for a few minutes.

LEADERSHIP LEARNING CONCEPTS

• Problem Solving

• Creative Thinking

• Values

SUPPORTING STANDARDS

This activity supports content standards in ELA—Speaking and Listening, ELA—Writing (Enrichment), Social Studies, and Service Learning (see pages 9–14 for details).

MATERIALS NEEDED

• "Would You Rather Questions" handout (page 138)

Getting Ready

Print one copy of the "Would You Rather Questions" handout and cut it into separate slips with one question on each. Consider the age and maturity of your group of students, and discard any questions that seem too difficult or mature. You may also want to write some "Would you rather?" dilemmas of your own and add them to the pile.

Activity

Have kids take turns pulling questions from a hat or bowl, reading them aloud, and giving their opinion. Before leaving each question, encourage others to share their opinions as well.

Alternatively, you can read the questions from the list aloud to the group, allowing responses and discussion before moving on to the next question.

Enrichment

After completing the activity with the questions included in the handout, have kids develop and share their own "Would you rather?" questions (keeping the focus on leadership and life situations rather than the general odd and gross type of questions typically found in "Would you rather?" games). Have students select and respond to the questions as you did with the regular activity.

WOULD YOU RATHER

Questions

Begin every question with "Would you rather . . ."

1. Volunteer at a homeless shelter or a nursing home?

2. Be captain of your sports team or a member only?

3. Be captain of a sports team or president of your class?

4. Travel to the moon or the center of the earth?

5. Be the smartest person in school or the most popular person in school?

6. Be an excellent writer or an excellent public speaker?

7. Discover a cure for cancer or a cure for the common cold?

8. Invent a hot new technology gadget that could make you millions or invent a method to purify water in poor countries that could save millions of lives?

9. Be rich and unhappy or poor and happy?

10. Run your own company or work for someone else?

11. Uncover a secret that accurately predicts natural disasters or be able to stop every war?

12. Speak any language in the world or know the answer to every question?

13. Play on teams with all your friends and win only 1 out of 5 games or play on a team with no one you know and win 4 out of 5 games?

14. Be the leader of your country or be an advisor to the leader of your country?

15. Have a friend take the blame for a bad choice you made together or take the blame for a friend?

16. Stand up to a bully or stand up to a teacher with whom you disagree?

17. Stop pollution or hunger?

18. Be famous but have few real friends or be mostly unknown but well-liked by everyone who meets you?

19. Only be able to whisper when you talk or only be able to shout?

20. Always have to say everything on your mind or never be able to speak?

21. Live without music or without video games?

22. Never get to watch TV again or never be able to use the Internet again?

MAGIC
Carpet*

As passengers on a magic carpet, the team works together to flip the carpet over during an imaginary flight through the air. A few leaders emerge in this activity requiring the rest of the group to follow.

Time: 15–20 minutes (depending on group size)

Age: Grades K–6

Group Size: No limit

LEADERSHIP LEARNING CONCEPTS

- Problem Solving
- Teamwork

SUPPORTING STANDARDS

This activity supports content standards in Math, and Health and Physical Education (see pages 9–14 for details).

MATERIALS NEEDED

- tarp (for groups of 10–12 you can use the 5' x 5' tarp from Zapping Maze on page 188; for larger groups, the large blue plastic tarps found at do-it-yourself hardware stores can fit up to 50 kids at a time. For groups in between, either cut or fold the large tarp to a smaller size)

*Contains modifications for students transitioning to middle school

Getting Ready

Lay the tarp flat on the ground. To determine the size of tarp to use, do a dry run by having all the kids in your group stand on the tarp. If everyone fits with a little space to move around, you have a good size, but if they have lots of space you may want to fold in one or more edges to make it smaller. In general, the smaller the tarp compared to the number of kids in the group, the greater the challenge in solving the problem.

You can divide a large group into multiple small groups, laying out a small tarp for each group of 10 to 12 kids. Because leaders typically emerge in this activity, having several small groups working simultaneously on separate tarps keeps more people engaged in the activity.

Activity

Ask everybody to step onto the tarp with both feet. Create an imaginary setting for the activity by explaining that they have all just stepped onto a magic carpet, and continue by saying:

> **You are now floating through the clouds. But something is wrong with the magic in your carpet! It seems to be coasting downward, and you realize it's upside down. In order to keep it floating, your entire team must turn the carpet over. To be successful, everyone needs to stay on the magic carpet while turning it over. If anyone steps off the magic carpet, they fall off and the group must start again. One other rule: Everyone must be touching the magic carpet at all times, so no lifting each other or jumping. Any questions?**

Answer any questions before saying "go." There is no time limit to this activity. Typically a few people step up as leaders. Because of this, some kids take a backseat and wait to be told what to do. This can cause frustration for some but also leads to success overall. Pay attention to the dynamics so you can point out when others are being overlooked and/or decide to add limitations or enhancements. Limitations and enhancements may include:

- no voice (for someone who is talking a lot)
- loss of vision (blindfolding someone who is getting bossy or agitated with others)
- two minutes of instant leadership (for someone who appears disengaged); requires others to listen to and follow this person (or group of people) for two minutes without interrupting
- floating (for someone who appears disengaged or is clearly frustrated); immediately allows them to "float" off the carpet for two minutes to advise the group from a distance

You may also increase the challenge for a group (best for older kids) by shrinking the size of the carpet at some point during the activity. Fold an end to make it smaller, and explain it like this:

> **Oh my! A gust of wind has just sheared off part of the magic carpet! Everyone must now move onto the remaining part and work from there. The same rules still apply.**

When the carpet has been turned completely over, celebrate the success. Ask everyone to sit down on the tarp for discussion.

Talk About It

Using terms your students will understand, ask questions like the following to help explore the leadership learning:

- What role did you play in this activity? Do you feel like you could have done more or less? Explain.
- Did some people act as leaders during the activity? How did they do that? How did you feel about the people who were your leaders?
- Did you feel like your ideas were listened to? Explain.
- Not everyone could be a leader in this activity. In what ways were the followers equally important?
- Did you agree with the method your group used to flip the carpet? Explain.
- How did you feel having to be so close to one another? What happens in real life when you find yourself in a similar situation?
- (If applicable) How did you feel when the magic carpet shrank because of the wind?

Middle School Transition Questions

If you are using this activity with fifth- or sixth-grade students who will be heading into middle school, consider including these questions during the discussion:

- Like being on the magic carpet when it is swept into the wind, life in middle school can be fun, magical—and sometimes a little scary. How can you take charge of your life when you feel like you're being pulled in the wrong direction?

- The magic carpet kept you safe as it floated along. You knew its boundaries. In middle school, what can you do to find a "safety zone" (socially, academically, with activities)? If you feel like you're out of your safety zone, what can you do to get back into it?

- In middle school you'll encounter unfamiliar situations and be faced with making new choices. Some will allow you to be a leader, while in others you may be a follower. If these choices or situations become dangerous or uncomfortable, are there others (mentors, leaders, peers) you can turn to for help?

- What can you do if something unexpected happens in your life (like the wind gust)?

- In what ways can you step up as a leader? Will it take anything special—a situation, a person asking, a cause—to get you to do this or are you willing to find ways to do it no matter what?

- How do you make sure others hear your views and ideas?

HUMPTY
Dumpty*

Small teams engage in creative thinking to build a contraption using limited resources that allows them to drop an egg from a certain height without letting the egg break.

Time: 45 minutes or longer (depending on group size); if time allows, you may choose to use an entire class period for building the contraptions and a second period for the presentations and drops

Age: Grades K–6

Group Size: No limit

Note: An alternative approach is to have groups work together outside of class time to create their contraptions and use session time to test them. While this session is primarily geared toward grades 3–6, see Variation for a version to use with grades K–2.

LEADERSHIP LEARNING CONCEPTS

- Creative Thinking
- Problem Solving
- Teamwork
- Resourcefulness

SUPPORTING STANDARDS

This activity supports content standards in ELA—Speaking and Listening, and Math (see pages 9–14 for details).

MATERIALS NEEDED

- 2–3 raw eggs for each group of three
- 20 plastic straws for each group of three
- 30-inch piece of masking tape for each group of three
- 2–4 large plastic garbage bags (or a plastic painter's tarp and one plastic garbage bag)
- chair or stepping stool
- Optional: two-piece plastic eggs (grades K–2 Variation)
- Optional: jelly beans or other small candies, paper clips, rubber erasers, or any weighty, unbreakable items (grades K–2 Variation)

*Contains modifications for students transitioning to middle school

Getting Ready

Collect and divide the eggs, straws, and masking tape into the designated quantities for each team of three kids. You will distribute them later.

Lay the plastic tarp out on the floor underneath and around a chair or stepping stool, or cut the seams of a couple garbage bags and lay them out as a tarp. Tape the edges of the bags or tarp to the floor so they don't slip when stepped on. Place the chair or stool on top and in the middle of the bags or tarp. This will be the "drop zone" for the raw eggs.

Activity

Ask the following questions to introduce creative thinking, problem solving, and teamwork:

- **What does it mean to think creatively?**
- **How many of you think you solve problems creatively? Give some examples.**
- **How many of you believe you don't really think creatively? Explain.**
- **Are artists the only ones who are creative? Why or why not?**
- **What sorts of things help you think creatively or keep you from thinking creatively?**

Allow a few minutes for discussion. If necessary, present the following broad view about creative thinking:

Thinking creatively is being able to come up with new ideas or deal with problems in fresh ways. Although creative thinking doesn't always come naturally, it is a skill you can develop with practice. You can even make creative thinking a positive habit. People sometimes believe they aren't creative thinkers because they get stuck on the words *creative* or *creativity*. They think creativity means painting, music, writing, and other artistic activities. But leaders use creative thinking to find unique ways to solve problems instead of doing things the same old way. Today, you'll explore how thinking creatively can help in leadership roles and when working as a team.

Divide participants into teams of three. Have each team find an area in the room to work undisrupted and uninfluenced by the other teams' ideas. Once teams are in place, recite the nursery rhyme "Humpty Dumpty":

Humpty Dumpty sat on a wall.
Humpty Dumpty had a great fall.
All the king's horses and all the king's men
Couldn't put Humpty together again.

Bummer for Humpty—he's in the hospital! While he recovers, the king is looking for a talented group to create a special contraption or tool that will protect Humpty Dumpty from this happening again. Your task is to create a case that will protect Humpty when he returns to his post on the wall after leaving the hospital. The contraption must be created *around* an egg, not as a target for an egg to land on. Each team will get the same materials to create its contraption. This is all you have to work with and you may not use any other materials or tools such as scissors, clippers, pens, pencils, hair bands, or other objects.

In addition to creating your contraption, pick a team name and choose a spokesperson from your team to promote your contraption to the king. Then, to prove your contraption works, your spokesperson will drop it from five or six feet off the ground (stand on the chair to illustrate), where it must land without the egg breaking. If more than one contraption works, the respective teams will re-drop the contraptions from higher heights to determine which is most successful. You have 25 minutes to create your contraption. Questions?

Answer any questions without giving hints about ways to create a contraption. If kids ask if they can use their body in any way (for example, their teeth to cut items), restate that they're to think creatively and avoid giving specifics in order to promote the freedom to use imagination and the on-hand resources (which includes their body). Remind them that the contraption is to be made around the egg, not as a landing pad and that there is no one right method or design. As long as kids follow the rules and the contraption works, they can make whatever they want. For one creative solution idea, see page 146.

Make sure the teams wait to begin until everyone has the materials and you begin timing. Pass out one egg (initially), 20 straws, and the 30" piece of masking tape to each team.

As you track the time, check in with each team and offer encouragement. If kids appear to be spying or copying the ideas of other teams, remind them that the goal is to think creatively and that the king is looking for a team that can solve problems in ways that haven't been thought of before. If any eggs break during the planning and building stage, allow each team at least one replacement. Emphasize that resources are limited to encourage participants to be careful with their eggs.

After 25 minutes, give each group spokesperson one to two minutes to share the team name, promote the contraption, and stand on the chair or stepping stool to drop it. If the egg remains unbroken, have the group hold onto it until the others take their turns. If no other eggs make it without breaking, congratulate the winning team. If other eggs also make it in one piece, have the successful teams take additional turns dropping the contraptions from greater heights until only one remains. Congratulate the winning team before moving onto discussion. Use the extra plastic bags to discard the broken eggs and bags taped to the floor.

If no contraptions are successful, take two to three minutes to have the group brainstorm which features of each contraption could be combined to possibly create a successful contraption before discussing the experience.

Talk About It

Using terms your students will understand, ask questions like the following to help explore the leadership learning:

- Explain what steps your teams took to 1) come up with the idea for your contraption; and 2) actually build your contraptions. (Allow each team to explain.)

- How did it feel to solve a problem using your imagination to find *any* solution rather than looking for only one exact solution?

- Was it hard to think creatively? Why or why not?

- Did anyone on your team get stuck thinking only one way? How did you deal with this?

- Can problem solving be fun? How so? (Get several replies and compare answers.) Do limited resources or restrictive rules make a difference? Why or why not?

- How is it possible for two different groups to come up with the same new idea?

- How can a leader or group members encourage creative thinking?

- Is being able to think creatively important to being an effective leader? Why or why not?

Variation

This variation can be better to use with kids in grades K–2, who lack the grace and coordination of older kids, because there are no raw eggs to make a mess. Conduct the session in the same way as described, replacing the real eggs with one plastic egg filled with weighty, unbreakable items (such as candy, paper clips, or rubber erasers). Clearly explain that teams cannot use their tape to seal the eggs together at the spot where they snap together. Using larger plastic eggs (similar in size or larger than real eggs) is preferable to using the smaller ones.

Middle School Transition Questions

If you are using this activity with fifth- or sixth-grade students who will be heading into middle school, take a few minutes to brainstorm "problems" they faced during elementary school and feel they've addressed creatively (such as dealing with bullies, time management for projects, switching schools, making new friends, or saying no to peer pressure).

Also brainstorm a list of "new" problems they anticipate could arise in middle school. Then, ask:

- When faced with solving old problems that resurface or new problems that arise in middle school, what will you do to think creatively about them?

- How will you deal with people who pressure you to follow their ideas even if you disagree with them?

- What have you learned about yourself so far in life about how you solve problems? Does this style work for you? If not, what will you change when you start middle school?

- When any of your new ideas fall flat, what will you do to learn from your mistakes?

One Solution to
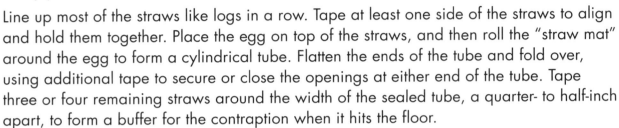

Here's a description and drawing of one possible design for "Humpty Dumpty." There is more than one solution to the activity.

Line up most of the straws like logs in a row. Tape at least one side of the straws to align and hold them together. Place the egg on top of the straws, and then roll the "straw mat" around the egg to form a cylindrical tube. Flatten the ends of the tube and fold over, using additional tape to secure or close the openings at either end of the tube. Tape three or four remaining straws around the width of the sealed tube, a quarter- to half-inch apart, to form a buffer for the contraption when it hits the floor.

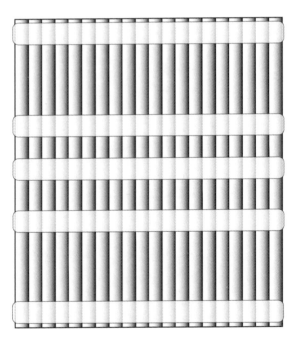
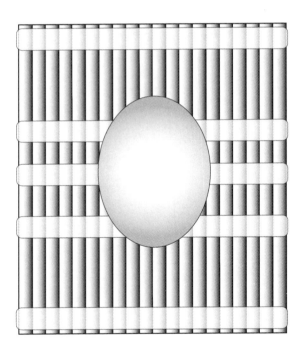

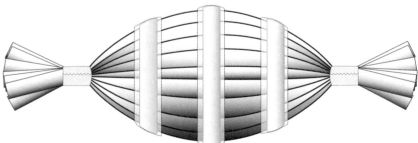

TIME CAPSULE
Transfer

The group must come up with a creative and sturdy way to move an elevated base holding a small can of items from the starting point to a safety zone. This activity can also be used to introduce basic physics concepts while still emphasizing leadership skills and teamwork.

Time: 30 minutes

Age: Grades 3–6

Group Size: Small groups of 10–12 work best

Note: Multiple groups can attempt the task one after the other, or have enough props for multiple groups to attempt the task simultaneously along different paths.

LEADERSHIP LEARNING CONCEPTS

• Problem Solving
• Resourcefulness
• Creative Thinking
• Communication

SUPPORTING STANDARDS

This activity supports content standards in ELA—Speaking and Listening, Math, and Health and Physical Education (see pages 9–14 for details).

MATERIALS NEEDED

• clean plastic "clamshell" container from berries (larger size—approximately 9½" x 11", give or take); there should be preexisting air holes in the top and bottom sections of the container (on the side is okay, too)

• sturdy string, rope, or twine (small enough to fit through the preexisting air holes of the plastic container, but not too small in diameter); another alternative is extra-long shoelaces (you'll need four 84" or longer shoelaces, such as from work boots, plus several shorter ones that serve as "distractions")

• empty coffee can or plastic container without lid (one-pound size or slightly larger; if it's too big, the filled can will be too heavy for the treasure platform)

- miscellaneous light-weight small items to fill the can including bouncy balls or ping pong balls, mid-sized soft balls, miniature stuffed animals or other stuffed toys, plastic cars, and so on
- milk crate or stool
- masking tape
- stopwatch or watch
- Optional: various objects to be obstacles on the path such as small construction cones, hula hoops, blocks, or chairs

Getting Ready

You need ample space to conduct this activity. It can be conducted outside.

Lay out a course the students will take to complete the task and tape down a start line and finish line. If conducting this activity outside, lay yardsticks or other stable items down to mark the start and finish lines. Make the distance between the starting line and the finish line approximately 25 to 40 feet. If you wish, you can place the various obstacles in the path from the starting point to the safety zone.

Cut the string or twine into at least four segments of 8 feet each. Then have as many other pieces as you want in lengths varying from 2 to 6 feet long. The shorter lengths can be used to support the transfer base, however the longer ones are necessary for the group to succeed with the transfer.

Collect the miscellaneous small items and put them inside the can. Place the full can at the starting location on top of the closed lid of the plastic berry container. Lay the string or twine in a pile nearby.

Activity

The objective of this activity is to transport the filled can on top of the berry container from the start of the course to the finish. Kids will need to run the strings through the holes in the plastic container in such a way as to support the weight of the can and prevent it from sliding or tipping off the top of it. Everyone in the group needs to be holding at least one piece of string as the time capsule is transported, and no one can touch the capsule or the plastic container while they're being moved. Each piece of string can be used to creatively bear weight or steady the can. Create a fun storyline to build a sense of urgency and importance for the task students are to complete. Here's one example:

Congratulations! You have discovered a time capsule filled with priceless artifacts. To find out the meaning of each artifact—and whether the time capsule has any messages that will change the world—you must first get your discovery to a nearby museum. The capsule and the transport box may not be touched by human hands or they will disintegrate! You have everything you need to achieve greatness. In order to complete this task, however, everyone must be holding a piece of string when you cross the finish line and place the transport box onto the research table (the stool or crate). If the can or strings are dropped at any time, you'll have to start again. (If using obstacles, you might add: If you run into any obstacles, you'll have to start again.) Your team can make a plan without taking any action as long as you want, but you have only 20 minutes total to get the box from start to finish. Any questions?

Answer any questions unless kids are asking strategy questions, then stop answering and encourage them to talk with one another. If necessary, remind the team that the only way to move forward is if everyone is holding onto an end of string. If any piece of the string is dropped, you must return to the starting point.

Start the clock as soon as the group begins strategizing. If they go beyond five to eight minutes of strategy time, suggest to them that it's time for action. Stop the activity after 20 minutes. If they haven't achieved the transport, allow the group to negotiate for more time.

This is a challenging exercise and some groups benefit from a bit of coaching along the way. If the group struggles to work out what to do, freeze the action and help them discuss.

If the group spills the time capsule entirely, make a big deal about its catastrophic loss, invite them to discuss what went wrong and how they can do better, then refill the container and have them start over.

Talk About It

Using terms your students will understand, ask questions like the following to help explore the leadership learning:

- Explain the strategy your team used for transporting the time capsule. How did your team agree on this strategy?

- Did you ever feel frustrated during the activity? If so, how did your team stay focused?

- What were some problems you ran into? When things didn't go as you hoped, how did your group handle it?

- Did anyone emerge as a leader? If so, how did that work for your group?

- How did you express your opinion if you disagreed with how the group was attempting to solve this problem?

- Did everyone get a chance to voice ideas? If not, what would you have changed?

- What would have made this problem easier to solve?

- Have you ever had to solve a problem with limited resources? Explain.

- How can you apply this activity to real life?

SESSION · SESSION · SESSION · SESSION

40

CHOOSE
a Flag

This activity introduces the idea of consensus or full-agreement decision making. To achieve the goal of the activity (choosing a team flag), the group must first select a team leader. The team leader then guides the group to choose its flag. Both decisions must be accomplished with everyone in agreement, rather than using majority rule (voting). Through the process, kids learn to voice their opinions (even though some are scripted), value the opinions of others, and compromise.

Time: 35 minutes

Age: Grades 3–6

Group Size: Groups of 15–20 work best

LEADERSHIP LEARNING CONCEPTS

- Decision Making
- Group Dynamics
- Problem Solving

SUPPORTING STANDARDS

This activity supports content standards in ELA—Speaking and Listening, Social Studies, and Service Learning (see pages 9–14 for details).

MATERIALS NEEDED

- large envelope (9" x 12")
- scissors, tape
- chairs
- "Label for Choose a Flag" handout (page 153)
- "Roles for Choose a Flag" handout (pages 154–155)

Getting Ready

If using chairs, arrange them in a circle. Otherwise, plan on having participants sit on the floor to form a circle. Make a copy of the "Label for Choose a Flag" handout (page 153) and cut out the label. Make one or two copies of the "Roles for Choose a Flag" handout (pages 154–155) and cut out the role slips so you have enough for everyone in your group except for the leader (which the group will choose). If you have fewer than 17 group members, exclude some of the slips, starting with the Observer roles and then the roles that appear more than once until you have one role slip for everyone except the leader.

Note: If you have a large group, perhaps more than 25 or 30, consider breaking it into two groups and conducting this activity with each group separately but simultaneously to keep from bogging down in negotiations and to ensure that everyone participates.

Tape the "Directions" label on the outside of the envelope. Fold the role play slips in half and insert them into the envelope.

Activity

Introduce the topic of decision making in general, and consensus or full-agreement in particular, by saying something like this:

> **Flipping a coin or cutting a deck of playing cards is often an easy way to make a decision when only one or two people are involved. But sometimes you're part of a group and many people want to be involved in making a decision. A lot of times, a group can simply vote, with the choice that gets the most votes becoming the winner. But in some situations, you need the entire group to agree. That's how you will decide for this activity—your entire group will have to agree on the color of its flag. This is called consensus or full-agreement, and as you can imagine, it's a lot harder to make a decision this way than flipping a coin or voting!**

Depending on your group, you may need to provide additional information, such as:

> **When a group tries to reach a decision by full-agreement, everyone in the group gets to express their opinion. But for the group's decision to be final, everyone must agree to it. You probably know more about majority rule, where everyone gets a vote and the majority preference wins. As**

> **familiar as that is, today your decision is only final once everyone in the group agrees.**

Have everyone sit in a circle. Explain that each person will be role-playing (define this term, if necessary). First, have the group select a leader. They can do this any way they want—as long as they all agree with the decision.

After a leader has been selected, hand him or her the envelope with the role slips inside and direct the leader to read aloud the instructions on the label. These instructions will describe the group's goal—to choose a flag color using consensus—and direct everyone to take a role slip from the envelope without looking at what the slip says until after they pick it. As the leader passes around the envelope for everyone to take out a slip of paper, reinforce that no one is to share what's written on the slips of paper they draw.

Ask for a volunteer who received an Observer role slip to be the timekeeper, and let the group know that they get 15 minutes to complete their task (choosing a flag color). Ask the timekeeper to give a warning when the group has one minute left. When the one-minute warning comes, if the group is having a hard time reaching a decision, you can also ask:

> **With where the group is now, is it possible for you to reach a decision if you are given two additional minutes?**

If the answer is "yes," allow the team another two minutes past the ending time to reach their decision. If the answer is "no," end the activity when time runs out. A "no" answer means kids are at a stalemate, something that can happen in unscripted consensus decision making. You can address this during discussion.

Before going on to the Talk About It questions, have everyone read their role slips aloud before you collect the envelopes and instructions. This allows the group to see how the dynamics were set up from the beginning.

Talk About It

Using terms your students will understand, ask questions like the following to help explore the leadership learning:

- When told the group was selecting a leader, did you want to be chosen or did you want the leader to be someone else?

- If you wanted to be leader, how did you make this known? How did you feel when the leader was chosen, especially since the entire group had to agree?

- (If applicable) When picking a leader, what did the group do when _____ (name of person) refused to compromise or negotiate?

- Do you think the descriptions on the role slips are accurate examples of how people act when an entire group tries to make a decision? Why or why not?

- How did you feel acting a way that was different from how you normally act in a group? If your slip told you to be disagreeable, was it harder or easier when the group got close to a decision? Why?

- When people in a group can't come to an agreement, what can a leader do to get them to agree?

- Why do you think time limits were set? How did everyone respond to these limits?

- (If the activity ended with a stalemate) When a group can't reach a decision because no one will budge from their position, it's called a stalemate. What would it have taken for your group to reach an agreeable decision?

- How would reaching a decision have been different if the final decision were *really* important? (For example, what if you were on a jury that would decide whether the person on trial went to jail?)

- How would this activity have been different if you could have voted to decide your flag color? How would you have felt if you were outvoted? What if the decision was based on a difference of only one or two votes?

- What are some important things to consider when choosing the decision-making strategy for a group to use? (Examples might include: how many people are in the group; how important the decision is; what will happen if everyone doesn't agree; and whether a vote takes into consideration every member of that group.)

Label for
CHOOSE A FLAG

Make a copy of the following label with directions and cut it out on the dotted lines.

Directions

Time Allowed: 15 minutes

Task: Choose a color for your team flag guided by your new leader. Before making a decision as a group, each member, except your new leader, is to take one of the small slips of paper from this envelope and follow the individual instructions. Don't let anyone see your instructions or tell anyone what they say. Your flag must be one color (it can't be a rainbow or designs with various colors). Your decision isn't final until EVERYONE AGREES.

Roles for
CHOOSE A FLAG

Make a copy of the following roles. Cut out the roles needed and insert them into the envelope.

- ✂

You believe everyone should be allowed to express his or her opinion. Make sure everyone gets his or her say throughout the decision process. You want the color blue.

- ✂

You dislike when people don't get along. When people disagree, suggest a new color option—any color.

- ✂

You like asking questions even if they are off topic. Ask a lot of questions and bring up other topics by saying things like, "That reminds me of . . ." You want the color red.

- ✂

You like trying to be helpful, sharing your opinion, and asking questions in order to reach a decision. You like any color except red.

- ✂

You like to be different and unique; you're known for being very creative. Introduce unusual colors, such as neon green or bright blue. You don't want any basic colors (like red, blue, or yellow).

- ✂

You're a follower and easily agree with others. You like yellow, but will also support any shade of green if it is introduced by someone else.

- ✂

You constantly give your opinion, whether or not people are listening; in fact, you talk all the time! You are against blue.

- ✂

You are a great team player. You don't prefer any color more than others, but you really dislike green. When it sounds like the group is close to a decision, you try to wrap things up.

- ✂

Roles for

(continued)

- ✂

You believe nothing gets done in groups. You prefer doing things yourself. You find something wrong with everyone's ideas, including any colors people suggest. Pick your own favorite color and stick with it.

- ✂

Although the group selected a leader, you act like you think you would be a better leader. For example, interrupt the leader or point out how your ideas are better. Whatever color the leader chooses, you ask for a specific shade. (For example, if the leader suggests or chooses "blue," you say, "light blue or dark blue? Or royal blue?")

- ✂

Although the group selected a leader, you act like you think you would be a better leader. For example, interrupt the leader or point out how your ideas are better. Say things like, "Well, if I were the leader—not that I want to be—I would suggest . . . " and give your own ideas.

- ✂

You are very uncomfortable when people disagree (unless someone suggests the color black, which is your least favorite color). You don't say much unless people are arguing without giving in; then you jump in to stop the conflict.

- ✂

You don't like any color in particular, say yes to everyone's ideas, and joke about the group's goal. Goof off and kid around to the point that others in the group can't take you seriously.

- ✂

You're an observer within the group. You watch what everyone in the group does. Don't speak with the others. If anyone asks for your opinion, avoid giving one or give a wishy-washy one.

- ✂

You're an observer within the group. You watch what everyone in the group does. Don't speak with the others. If anyone asks for your opinion, avoid giving one or give a wishy-washy one.

- ✂

You're an observer within the group. You watch what everyone in the group does. Don't speak with the others. If anyone asks for your opinion, avoid giving one or give a wishy-washy one.

- ✂

Understanding POWER, VALUES, and RELATIONSHIPS

The interplay of power, values, and relationships is a complex and challenging concept to grasp. Kids recognize who has power in their groups, but may struggle with why or how that person has gained that power. The same is true of understanding the role and importance of values, both individually and within a group context. The activities in this section emphasize deeper inquiry, which leads to discussions and real-life application that require higher-order abstract thinking. For this reason, most of these activities are designed for kids in grades 3 and up. One activity does fit all ages, and a Variation for What's It Worth? also can be used with grades K–2.

Contains modifications for students transitioning to middle school

157

SESSION · SESSION · SESSION · SESSION

41

SMIRK*

Teams compete to gain members by trying to get the opposing team to smile or laugh. While presenting a simple, humorous way to challenge the ability of individual young leaders to stand their ground, the exercise also requires strength as a team. Take time afterward to talk about peer pressure and its influence on individuals and groups. Having the discussion before the activity can diminish some of its impact, so wait until after completing the activity to make the peer pressure connection.

Time: 35 minutes

Age: Grades K–6

Group Size: No limit

Note: Even-numbered groups work best for this activity. You can have multiple small groups of 16–20 doing the activity simultaneously. If you have an odd number of kids, give one team an additional member, or if your group is grades 5–6, the additional participant can serve as the referee (instead of the teacher).

LEADERSHIP LEARNING CONCEPTS

• Bullies, Cliques, and Peer Pressure

• Teamwork

• Goal Setting

SUPPORTING STANDARDS

This activity supports content standards in ELA—Speaking and Listening, Social Studies, and Service Learning (see pages 9–14 for details).

MATERIALS NEEDED

• open space to set up teams in two lines, with room between the lines for two individuals to walk

• Optional: joke book (Variation)

• Optional: pens, loose-leaf paper, and chart paper (Enrichment)

*Contains modifications for students transitioning to middle school

Getting Ready

Depending on the space you are using to conduct this activity, move any tables, chairs, or desks out of the way to create an open area for movement. Also, be prepared with a method of dividing your larger group into two smaller teams without allowing participants to select their own teammates. See page 5 for suggestions.

For groups where kids have physical challenges requiring crutches or a wheelchair, this activity can still be conducted as described; it may require a larger space for movement. Or, conduct the activity using the Variation on page 160, which requires no moving around.

Activity

This activity has two parts. For the first part, you give instructions and the teams and individuals proceed with no additional discussion or planning. For the second part, the teams repeat this activity, this time giving teams a few minutes to strategize before starting. Conduct the discussion only after both parts of the activity have been completed.

Divide the entire group into two teams and have them stand in parallel lines facing each other. Allow enough space so two kids can walk side by side between the two lines without touching each other or anyone in the lines. Explain the goal of the activity by saying:

Each line is a team. Every time I say "go," two people—one from each team—will walk together down the space between the two teams while those of you on the sidelines try to get the walkers to smile. You can do anything you want as long as it is appropriate for this group and you do not touch them or create any dangerous or awkward situations for either of them. If your team members make it to the finish without smiling, they stay on your team. But if they smile before finishing, the other team gets to add them to their line.

Everyone will take a turn walking down the line. The goal is to keep all the team members you started with and add as many as you can from the other team.

Since kids will want to try creative ways to get others to smile, you may want to explain what behaviors are appropriate:

- silly faces
- nonoffensive gestures
- funny sounds or movements
- jokes or riddles the entire group will find funny (If the whole group starts laughing, it's quite

difficult for the two walking down the middle not to find humor in the joke!)

Set guidelines and discourage the following:

- demeaning comments
- inside jokes, since others in the group may infer that such jokes involve them
- if kids in your group speak multiple languages, remind them that if they use a language unfamiliar to others in the group, they must still maintain decorum in their comments

After explaining the rules, identify the starting and ending points. Ask the first person from each line to step to the middle of the two lines at the starting point. When you say "go," this first pair begins walking down the line. Keep an eye out to make sure the pathway remains safe (such as making sure each team keeps hands and feet to themselves). Once they've made it to the end, have them rejoin their team or move to the other one, depending on whether they smiled. When everyone has passed through the line the first time, declare a winner if one team has grown. Then reassign everyone to their original teams and say:

Now that you've made it through, you will have another chance to increase your team numbers. This time, before sending members down the line, you will have five minutes to make a plan as a team. Then you'll line up again and take turns walking in pairs from the start to the finish, trying not to smile before you reach the end.

Allow five minutes for team strategizing and then conduct the process as before. When everyone has gone through the lines, count the team members and declare the winning team.

Talk About It

Be sure to talk about the ways strategizing takes place when there is peer pressure in everyday life. If necessary, share an example, such as when two people plan to persuade others in their group to agree to certain activities or ideas. For a social studies or service learning setting, see the Enrichments for ways to use historical examples such as genocides and racism to explore the sociological impact of peer pressure. Using terms your students will understand, ask questions like the following to help explore the leadership learning:

- What was it like when it was your turn to walk between the lines? Was it hard not to smile or laugh? Why or why not?

- What did your team do to help your teammates make it through to the other end? Was your team more focused on making the other team's members smile or on helping your own team members be successful? Explain.

- How did you feel when you couldn't make it to the other end without smiling?

- How did it feel to make one of the walkers smile?

- How was the experience different when your team was able to make a plan? How was it the same? What were some strategies you came up with? Did everyone agree to all the strategies? Were there any ideas that made you uncomfortable? Explain.

- How is this activity like real-life situations where others are pressuring you to do something you don't want to do?

- How do you help keep yourself focused on what's important to you so you can stand up for what you feel is right?

Middle School Transition Questions

If you are using this activity with fifth- or sixth-grade students who will be heading into middle school, consider including these questions during the discussion:

- What expectations do you have about handling peer pressure during middle school?

- How can you remain confident at making good decisions in middle school, especially if others are making decisions with which you disagree

(such as skipping classes, not studying for a test, or being disrespectful to others)?

- What are some things you can say when others are pressuring you to do something that goes against your values?

- How do you speak up against peer pressure and deal with friends who may choose different paths?

Variation

This activity can also be conducted by creating two lines seated on opposite sides of a table. Using a joke book or another funny resource, each team is allowed to tell their chosen joke to the person from the other team whose turn it is to "walk the line." As each opposing pair's turn comes up, they step to the head of the table to receive their joke from the other team. The opposing team can act out the joke or make funny noises or make funny faces to accompany the joke. The goal is the same—to get the individual to smile or laugh.

Enrichments

1. Encourage kids to take time outside the group to observe their role in situations that involve peer pressure. Encourage them also to notice how they react to or are influenced by peer pressure, both positive and negative. If time allows at the next group meeting, ask teens to share what they observed about themselves, their roles, and the pull of peer pressure in their lives.

2. If using this activity as a middle school transition activity, explore the pros and cons of peer pressure, and guide a general discussion about peer pressure. Divide the group into smaller groups of three or four. Pass out a piece of loose-leaf paper and pen to each group; ask kids to write the heading "Positive" on one side of the paper and "Negative" on the other. Have the small groups brainstorm examples of positive and negative peer pressure, writing their comments on the appropriate side. Then ask groups to share their examples. You may want to have a volunteer

write the entire list on a dry-erase board or large piece of chart paper. With the lists in front of the large group, conduct a discussion that addresses ways middle school students can appropriately manage negative peer pressure situations and ways they can engage in positive peer pressure.

3. Examine peer pressure in the larger world. For more mature groups (grades 5–6) or kids of all ages who live in complicated communities (for example, with high rates of violence, substance abuse, wealth without family parameters, domestic instability, poverty, racial inequity, or high social pressure), introduce the terms *groupthink* and *moral independence* (see next column) and have kids brainstorm examples of each. You can encourage them to think historically and globally so they can consider issues such as war, oppression of groups or individuals (genocides or censorship), substance use and abuse, physical and emotional bullying, cyberbullying, gang recruitment and activity, cults, and other situations where peer pressure plays a positive or negative role.

More About Peer Pressure, Groupthink, and Moral Independence

With kids in grades K–2, the discussion can revolve around positive and negative peer pressure. Positive peer pressure is when group members or individuals are able to persuade others around them to do things that have positive outcomes (such as participating in service projects, striving to get good grades, or refraining from littering). Negative peer pressure is when group members or individuals persuade others around them to do things that have negative outcomes (such as bullying, cheating, skipping school, or drinking alcohol).

Kids in grades 4–6, tweens, and young teens may feel that they readily resist peer pressure and so the topic may seem juvenile to them. In this case, you may want to focus on the concepts of groupthink and moral independence. Consider these definitions to frame the activity and subsequent discussions:

Groupthink

This occurs when members of a group begin thinking alike to the point that they may not consider other alternatives for their situation or decision. Groupthink can be interpreted in the positive as consensus and overall agreement. It can be negative when groups overlook making sound or safe decisions because they have started thinking very narrowly or have begun valuing the opinions and guidance of a select few. In these cases, group members may exert tremendous pressure on others in order to get them to agree with a certain decision or outcome.

- Strutting, dancing, or excessively celebrating with your sports team in front of your opponent when your team scores (negative)
- Getting a group of friends together to participate in Make a Difference Day or group volunteer activities, even if it's a new experience for them (positive)
- Cyberbullying by group text or email (negative)
- Organizing a group of student leaders to meet with your principal about fair or unfair school rules (positive)

Moral Independence

This is when members of a group are still fully capable of acting as individuals, even in the context of highly pressured group situations. Acting with moral independence means one is able to live by what is true, even if others, even the whole group, stand opposed. Moral independence is exhibited when others are trying to convince someone to do something that is not consistent with the person's beliefs, and the person stands firm for what she or he believes is right. Here are some examples:

- Confronting a bully when others around you do nothing
- Speaking up against a racist joke when others around you are laughing
- Picking an unpopular or nonathletic kid first for your team during playground picks

SESSION · SESSION · SESSION · SESSION

42

MORE LIKE ME*

Exploring values helps strengthen kids' understanding that not everyone shares the same views. These early conversations provide a natural segue into future discussions and experiences related to tolerance, stereotypes, empathy, and compassion. In this activity, kids consider which of two terms (representing individual values) better describes them, then stand on an imaginary line to represent their stance.

Time: 30–40 minutes, with discussion (longer with larger group sizes)

Age: Grades 3–6

Group Size: No limit

LEADERSHIP LEARNING CONCEPTS

- Values
- Self-Awareness

SUPPORTING STANDARDS

This activity supports content standards in ELA—Speaking and Listening, ELA—Language, Social Studies, and Service Learning (see pages 9–14 for details).

MATERIALS NEEDED

- masking tape
- "Sample Words for More Like Me" handout (page 166 for grades 3–6 version; page 167 for grades K–2 version)
- space to move around

*Contains modifications for students transitioning to middle school

Getting Ready

Make one copy of the appropriate "Sample Words for More Like Me" handout for your own use. Depending on the space being used to conduct this activity, move any tables, chairs, or desks out of the way to create an open area for movement. Tape a line of masking tape down the middle of the floor.

This activity can also be conducted outside.

For groups where kids have physical challenges requiring crutches or a wheelchair, this activity can still be conducted as described; it may require a larger space for movement.

Activity

Read the handout and choose several word pairs that work best for your group and time limit. You may want to add to or modify the list depending on maturity level and setting. With younger students, you may be inclined to use the simpler terms on the list; keep in mind that when youngsters think metaphorically, their deeper critical thinking skills are developed.

Prior to conducting the activity, you might want to introduce the topic of values with a brief discussion such as this:

- **What are some things (such as people, places, things you believe, and celebrations) that are important to you?**

- **Why are they important to you?**

- **Does anyone know what these "things" are called?**

These are called "values." Values are the things (people, what we believe, places, stuff, and so forth) that are important to each of us. We may share the same values as our friends or we may not. Let me give you a simple example:

Living in the city is important to me. Living on a farm is important to my best friend.

When you are older, some of the values you have right now will stay the same. But don't be surprised if some of your values change as you get older or you get involved in different activities or with different friends.

It's important to know your values because when you understand exactly how you feel about something, making decisions can be easier. This also helps you understand more about where other people, such as your friends, are coming from when they say something or act in ways that are different from what you would say or do.

Remember that values are like opinions—they are very personal, and not everyone shares the same ones. Facts, on the other hand, are those things that everyone agrees are true, such as a red light means you have to stop at an intersection. (Ask for examples of opinions and facts to affirm the difference between the two.)

The last thing to keep in mind about values is that the word is part of another word: "valuable." So, think how you would respond if someone offered you a million dollars to "buy" any of your values. By selling them, you'd no longer have them in your life. Would it be worth it to you to sell any of them? (Invite responses from kids.)

The pairs of words used in this activity are designed to concretely guide kids to understand how they might share similar values with friends, classmates, teammates but how they may express them in different ways.

Regardless of age, peer pressure can be an issue in this activity, even if kids don't realize they are feeling "pressured" to stand on a certain spot of the continuum. You may want to talk about how knowing one's values can help people resist pressure put on them by someone else to make a choice they might not agree with. (For another activity on the topic of peer pressure, see Smirk, page 158.)

The Enrichments at the end of the activity highlight ways to further explore personal values or to have older students develop a "values line" to use with peers or younger kids.

Ask kids to stand near the masking tape line. Explain the activity by saying something like this:

This line represents the difference between two choices. I'm going to read pairs of words or phrases. For each pair, one end of the line stands for the first word or phrase, and the other end represents the second one. Listen to the words and decide which word sounds more like you—that is, the word that better matches your personality or who you are. Then decide where to stand along the line to show which idea you value and how much you value it. For example, if I were to say "farm/city," you'll decide whether to stand closer to the "farm" end or the "city" end. If you stand on the farm end, you are saying that you are more like a farm than a city, or you like farms

better than cities. The closer you stand to one end of the line or the other, the stronger you relate to that word.

Stand anywhere on the line as long as you can explain why you are standing on that spot. Some of the pairs of words are so different you may find it's easy to pick one of the ends. With other pairs of words, you'll find it's harder to choose one end or the other. The middle of the line represents "It depends on the situation." Unless your beliefs really "depend on the situation," avoid standing in the middle because I want you to make a clear choice.

Answer any questions or clarify the activity for kids who are having difficulty understanding the concept. Once everyone is clear, slowly read each pair of words. Allow time for kids to move along the line to their spots. Take one to two minutes after each pair of words to invite kids to explain why they made the choice they did. Encourage all kids to speak up by attentively inviting different kids for their explanations.

It's sometimes helpful to ask kids what the words mean to them, beyond the simplest definitions. For example, consider the pair "player/coach." A player could be viewed as someone who works hard on the field and uses his or her skills and talents to get the "job" done (whether it's sports or otherwise); or a player could mean that person prefers to follow directions rather than give them. Being a coach can be viewed as someone who likes to inspire others to do well, uses his or her experience to lead a team, and likes seeing the big picture of the team or game; or being a coach could mean he or she likes to tell others what to do.

Only read as many pairs as are appropriate for the maturity and interest level of your group. Once you have finished reading the list of words, have kids sit where they are to discuss the activity.

Talk About It

Using terms your students will understand, ask questions like the following to help explore the leadership learning:

- What pairs of words on this list really made you think? Why?

- What other pairs of words would you put on the list? Explain.

- Think about a time when most of the group was at one end, but you were at the other. How did it feel to be one of the few people at the other end?

- When it seems like everyone shares the same beliefs, how can you help people with different beliefs feel included?

- Are there situations where your friends or family expect you to act a certain way (or believe a certain thing), even though you feel very differently? Explain.

- What sorts of situations in life may test your values the most? How do you think you'll handle these situations?

Middle School Transition Questions

If you are using this activity with fifth- or sixth-grade students who will be heading into middle school, consider including these questions during the discussion:

- What do you think it will be like to go to a school where you are meeting new people who may or may not share the same views or values as you?

- What sort of first impression do you want to make when meeting people who don't know you or your personality from elementary school?

- How might your opinions, views, or values change during middle school? What or who might influence you?

- Are you comfortable speaking up for yourself when necessary? What can you do to be more comfortable speaking up, especially if friends are pressuring you to do or say something with which you don't agree?

- How do you know whether it's better to be flexible about your values or to stand your ground? How do you envision yourself acting in each of these cases?

Enrichments

1. Have kids read (or read aloud to the group) the picture book *Purplicious* by Elizabeth Kann and Victoria Kann, which has a distinct tone of bullying and negative peer pressure. Have kids discuss and explore how it feels to be the only one with a certain view and what it can take, at times, to stand up for your beliefs.

2. If you have access to teenage leaders, this is a great activity to invite them to conduct it in lieu of an adult. Have them create a brief presentation or discussion about values, relating the topic to things kids find important in their lives right now; avoid having them look too far into the future. Once they have designed their list of word pairs and a brief discussion outline, have teens conduct the activity with your group of kids.

3. Have kids interview someone older than themselves (such as a parent, grandparent, or coach) about how the person's values have changed and what sorts of things influenced the changes.

4. Have older kids (grades 5–6) write a persuasive essay on the values that are most important to them. Depending on the setting, have each child present his or her essay as a speech. Allow time for others to ask questions and/or share their own story related to values that are expressed.

Sample Words for More Like Me (GRADES 3-6)

- Talker/Listener
- Bookstore/Library
- New York/Montana
- City/Country
- Saver/Spender
- Sudoku/Video games
- Coach/Player
- Tigger/Eeyore
- Watcher/Doer
- Fast/Slow
- Leader/Follower
- Art/Math
- Recess/Study hall
- Risk taker/Cautious
- Soccer/Chess
- Physical/Mental
- Rainbow/Pot of gold
- Journey/Destination

- Highway/Dirt road
- Hybrid car/Luxury car
- Walking/Running
- Read the book/Watch the movie
- Clean room/Messy room
- Organized/Cluttered
- Agree/Disagree
- Build/Invent
- Following plans or directions/ Flexible, creative
- Tree/Roots
- Ending/Beginning
- Outcome/Foundation
- Chihuahua/Labrador
- Use your hands/Use your mind
- Go camping/Stay at a hotel
- High-tech/Low-tech

Sample Words for More Like Me (GRADES K-2)

- Talker/Listener
- Organized/Messy
- Play outside/Play inside
- Lots of friends/One best friend
- Video games/Books
- Live in the city/Live in the country
- Learn by doing/Learn by listening
- Roller coaster/Merry-go-round
- Watch a movie/Act in a play
- Go camping/Stay in a hotel
- Summer/Winter
- Fast/Slow
- Watcher/Doer

43

INSIDE

Out*

This activity uses role playing scenarios to reinforce how simple actions can make a huge impact on the people feeling excluded by others. It provides an effective and sensitive way to bring real-life attitudes and behaviors into focus. Often, kids who are excluded by others in daily life quickly recognize the emotions and attitudes taking place in this activity. Kids who exclude others in real life, who are members of cliques known for being exclusive, or who act as bullies, often don't make a personal connection right away. It's important to address these exclusionary or bullying behaviors during the discussion.

Time: 30–45 minutes (depending on number of small groups)

Age: Grades 3–6

Group Size: No limit

LEADERSHIP LEARNING CONCEPTS

- Bullies, Cliques, and Peer Pressure
- Self-Awareness
- Tolerance and Diversity

SUPPORTING STANDARDS

This activity supports content standards in ELA—Speaking and Listening, Social Studies, and Service Learning (see pages 9–14 for details).

MATERIALS NEEDED

- "Inside-Out Role Plays" handout (page 172)
- chairs that can be placed together tightly in a circle

Contains modifications for students transitioning to middle school

Getting Ready

If your whole group consists of 10 to 12 kids, have everyone participate as one team. Otherwise, divide larger groups into smaller groups of 6 to 12 kids.

When dealing with multiple small groups, it is wise to determine how you'll divide the larger group into those smaller groups prior to the meeting. See page 5 for suggestions. These smaller groups will do the activity separately but simultaneously. Try to make each group comprised of a diverse set of kids. As much as possible, avoid having friends together to prevent their existing relationships from intensifying this activity and possibly reflecting exclusionary behaviors they may already engage in with peers.

Make one copy of the "Inside-Out Role Plays" handout for each group and read all three scenarios prior to conducting the activity to fully understand them. Organize the chairs into close circles, each with enough chairs for all but one member of a small group. If possible, have extra chairs available somewhere in the room. Decide which student you will have play the role (or roles) of "outsider" prior to conducting the activity.

Note: Carefully consider who you select to play the role of an outsider for each group. This needs to be someone who can deal with being excluded—left out or ignored—as well as included. Choose someone you know will be comfortable with others saying rude or unkind things toward him or her as part of the role play, and who is able to discern that others may say some things that aren't true but could be hurtful if expressed in real life.

It is tempting to call on individuals who often exclude others to serve as these outsiders. This can be effective, but it can also backfire. On the one hand, volunteers may have their eyes opened through the experience as they learn to feel empathy. On the other hand, kids may become aggressive and overly mean toward such a volunteer because of how they feel in real life. If this happens, it can lead to a situation in which the volunteer shuts down and overlooks any connection to their own daily behavior.

Also, some kids appear exclusionary when in fact they are extremely shy. If a shy child were to take the outsider role, the activity could backfire by causing the person to feel so exposed that she or he would be unable to engage in the role playing. In general, it is best to select a volunteer who can withstand being the object of both negative and positive attitudes.

Activity

The group (or groups) will role-play three scenarios in this activity, each with the outsider being excluded to a different degree. Conduct all three scenarios before discussing what occurred during any of the role playing.

Divide participants into the small groups you established. Open the activity by saying:

Each group is going to role-play three different situations that deal with someone being excluded, or left out, of the group. In order to do this, I am going to choose an individual in each group who'll play the role of an outsider for the activity.

Select the outsiders and ask those students to step out of the room for a few minutes where they can't hear the instructions you're going to give the remaining kids. Tell the groups:

In your small groups, you're going to role-play that you are a group of friends. I'll give you written instructions for role-playing three different situations, or scenarios. Do not share these with the others when they return. When the volunteers come back in the room, I will give them spoken instructions to become part of your groups. Then you will begin with Scenario A. You can do what you need to do to make the outsiders feel excluded, but don't go overboard. Avoid raising your voices and do not touch one another or say mean, personal things that could be taken for real. I'll let you know when it's time to move to Scenario B and when it's time to move on to Scenario C. You can look at the handout as much as you need, just don't let the outsider read it until we're done with all the scenarios.

Read the three scenarios aloud and then give each group the handout. Provide a few minutes for each group to review the scenarios (perhaps reading them out loud again) and ask questions before inviting all of the outsiders back into the room. Have each outsider stand near the group they started with and explain their role:

You're going to play outsiders to your group. Remember, this is just pretend and anything said to you by the group is not real. The groups have been given three different ways to act, and they may or may not let you become part of their group. They will not share the instructions they've been given with you. Your goal is to join the circle in which the entire group is sitting. For example, try talking with them, leaning into the group or convincing individuals to let you in. No one is to push, shove, or use other physical force. Also, everyone is to avoid raising their voice, but discussion, persuasion, and negotiation are all great ways to try to get in. Any questions?

Allow a few minutes for questions before asking every group to begin with Scenario A. After three to five minutes of role-playing, announce that the group should move on to Scenario B. Once more, after three to five minutes of role-playing Scenario B, announce that the group should move on to Scenario C. Allow the activity to end after groups have role-played Scenario C for five minutes.

When all scenarios are completed, have everyone sit in their small circles for the discussion.

Talk About It

Point out that the last scenario (C) leaves the groups with a friendly rapport, but anyone who was an outsider during the other scenarios will remember what it was like to be excluded. Because these scenarios are indicative of interactions that occur often among kids and tweens, ask students to share any situations in which they've experienced similar scenarios (as the excluders, the excluded, or one who strives to include others) in real life. Then, using terms your students will understand, ask questions like the following to help explore the leadership learning:

- How many of you have been excluded from a group? What was it like? How did you deal with it? (Tell students not to name names or identify anyone who excluded them.)

- For those of you who were outsiders in the role plays, how did each situation feel? If this were real life, how would you feel or think about yourself and about others?

- For those of you in the groups, what did it feel like to exclude someone? Do you think people always know when they're excluding others? Explain.

- If you see people excluding others, what can you do to make them realize what they're doing?

- Be honest, and raise your hands if you think you exclude others from your real-life groups. Can anyone volunteer to share why you think you do this? Do you think your behavior will change after today?

- In real life, what happens when people pretend to accept someone into their group but ignore or put down the person? What might happen if a person is constantly rejected or excluded?

- Is it possible that *some* people who bully others were at one time excluded from a group? Explain. How do you think this type of situation should be dealt with?

- What can you use from this activity to help you change your own behavior in everyday life?

Middle School Transition Questions

If you are using this activity with fifth- or sixth-grade students who will be heading into middle school, consider including these questions during the discussion:

- What can you do when you enter middle school to find a group of friends with whom you're comfortable?

- What can you do if you discover your group of friends is excluding, bullying, mocking, or otherwise putting down others?

- How easy is it for you to speak up when you see someone treating others poorly? What if the person doing the bullying is the "leader" of your group and you fear you'll be cast out or picked on after speaking up?

- What steps can you take so you feel confident, even in difficult situations, speaking up on behalf of yourself or someone else?

- While it may feel like you should be able to deal with a lot of things on your own once you enter middle school, do you still have an adult to whom you can turn if you find yourself in a tough situation (either being excluded or being part of a group that excludes others)? If not, how do you find someone like that, especially in middle school?

Enrichment

Have kids spend the next few days observing different situations where they see people being excluded (or find themselves intentionally or unintentionally excluding others). Take time during your next meeting to express and commit to ways they can change their behavior if they're excluding others or if they witness exclusion but don't feel comfortable confronting it.

INSIDE-OUT
Role Plays

Scenario A

In this situation, your circle of friends will keep your backs to the outsider and completely exclude him or her from your group. When that person tries to join your group, move closer to each other or give the person a disapproving look. You can say things in a snarky tone, but do not say hurtful things that could be taken as if you really mean them. Do not call others names or comment on their appearance or body or personal things you may know about them. Here are examples of what you might say:

- "Isn't it annoying when people don't get the hint that they aren't welcome?"

- "Maybe we should meet somewhere else where people can't butt in."

- "I wish we could just choose who'll be members (friends) of this group and not worry about others trying to join us."

Scenario B

When the time comes to move into Scenario B, you can say something like: "Oh, hi, (person's name). I didn't see you there. Come sit with us!" In this situation, your circle of friends will physically let the outsider into your group. You can do this by making room in your circle and sharing a chair or by bringing another chair into the group for the person. Once you've invited the outsider in, though, ignore the person. Speak to one another and to anyone else except the outsider. Barely pay attention to the new person and change the topic if the outsider says anything or tries to join the conversation.

Scenario C

When the time comes to move into Scenario C, you can say something like, "Hey, (name of person), you've been trying to share your ideas this whole time. We'd love to hear what you think." In this situation, your circle of friends will truly include the outsider and try to make the person feel welcome. You are to invite him or her into your conversation, asking questions and inviting ideas from that person. Respond sincerely to the person's comments. If you want, you can apologize for excluding the person and explain that you didn't realize how much you have in common.

44

WHAT'S IT Worth?

Kids rank a list of personal values, and using play money (or tokens) bid against others to win the ones that mean the most to them. Multiple quantities of some values are available, while others are "limited edition." Kids learn to examine their values and personal priorities as well as negotiate with their peers.

Time: 30 minutes

Age: Grades 3–6

Group Size: No limit

LEADERSHIP LEARNING CONCEPTS

- Values
- Discernment
- Communication

SUPPORTING STANDARDS

This activity supports content standards in ELA—Speaking and Listening, Math, Social Studies, and Service Learning (see pages 9–14 for details).

MATERIALS NEEDED

- "Values for Sale" handout (page 176)
- several copies of the "Paper Money" handout (page 178)
- Optional: plastic coins or plastic chips (like poker or bingo chips)
- Optional: interactive whiteboard
- Optional: "Values for Sale" blank template handout (page 177) for Variation

Getting Ready

Read through the "Values for Sale" handout and decide how many of each value you want to make available for purchase. The total number you choose can be based on the number of kids in your group as well as which of the values you believe may be more popular (for example, feeling safe, having a family when old enough, making a positive difference) or relevant to your community culture. You may also add up to three values on the blank lines at the bottom of the handout if you choose. Write the number available of each value in the left-hand column beside the list. If you will offer only one of each value, mark a "1" and mention this when explaining the activity.

Make a copy of the "Values for Sale" handout with your quantities filled in for each child. If using an interactive whiteboard, display a copy of the list as well. Make several copies of the paper money handout—enough so that you can distribute to each student a pack of $1,000 made up of all denominations of bills. Cut the bills from the handouts and create the $1,000 packs for each student.

If you are using coins or chips instead of the paper money (see Variation), assign a value to each color or size and divide accordingly to achieve $1,000.

Activity

Lead a discussion with your group about what values are: A value is something that is important to you or an expectation of how you will behave or treat others. Pass out a copy of the "Values for Sale" handout with quantities to every kid, and urge kids to think about which of these values are most important to them. You may choose to go through the list of values one by one to be sure every child understands each one.

Pass out the money or chips. Explain the activity like this:

> **You are about to enter an auction to purchase the values that are most important to you. Everyone has $1,000. You can spend as much or as little as you want to purchase your values. Before we begin the bidding, take five minutes to rank your priorities and write how much you are willing to spend for each value. Remember, you cannot spend more than $1,000 total. Once the items are sold, you will write how much it sold for, either to you or someone else.**

> **(If applicable) You'll see that some values have more than one available to purchase. I will run multiple auctions for these values until all of them have been bought. You may get that value for more or less than someone else pays for it.**

> **Highest bidder gets the value and once it's gone, it's gone. Any questions?**

Make sure everyone understands the activity and all of the values on the list. Discuss anything that is unclear. You may want to discuss rules for the auction. Kids will need to manage their own money supply so that if they win a bid, they do indeed have the money to pay for it. Explain how you will accept bids—you might want to use hand gestures instead of vocal bids to prevent shouting as kids get excited. You may also want to go over how bids end ("going once, going twice, sold").

Answer any other questions before providing five minutes for kids to rank and organize their value list and budget. When everyone is ready, conduct a brisk auction, starting each value at $25 and allowing kids to move the number up in increments of $25 or more. Collect the appropriate money after each sale.

Talk About It

Using terms your students will understand, ask questions like the following to help explore the leadership learning:

- How happy are you with the values you won? Explain.

- What value did you not win and wish you had?

- Now that the auction is over, are there any values you won that you'd give up to get a different one?

- Which values would you keep, no matter how much money someone offered you?

- Have your values ever been challenged in real life, such as when another person disagrees with what you value, tells you your value is "wrong" or "bad," or tries to convince you to believe or do something else? (Some examples include a vegetarian staying quiet when eating with friends who eat meat, or on the flip side, being urged to eat meat despite his or her value; choosing to say the "Pledge of Allegiance" or not; or deciding to join a certain club or sports team despite friends urging you to join another.)

- Who are the most important people who guide your values?

- What do you do when your values are different from your friends' values and this difference causes disagreements (conflict)?

- Do you think your values will change as you grow up? Explain.

Variation

If your group is in a setting that reflects different or additional values from those represented on the list, conduct the activity using the template on page 177, and lead a values brainstorm session with your group prior to the auction to develop your own list. Ask kids to brainstorm all of the things that are important in their lives. You may need to explain what values and priorities are (see the More Like Me activity on page 162 for a sample explanation). After completing the brainstorm, list the values on the dry-erase board or display them on an interactive whiteboard before conducting the auction as previously described.

VALUES for Sale

# Available	Value	Worth to Me	Actual Cost
	Having kids when I'm old enough		
	Owning a home		
	Having a good job		
	Being famous		
	Having a job I love		
	Doing well in school		
	Practicing my religion		
	Serving in the military		
	Getting married when I'm old enough		
	Going to college		
	Having "stuff"		
	Being a good athlete		
	Having a lot of friends		
	Being healthy		
	Making a lot of money		
	Being popular		
	Looking good		
	Inventing something important/useful		
	Finding a cure to a disease		
	Traveling		
	Being respected by others		
	Being a role model or mentor to others		
	Volunteering		
	Making a positive difference in the world		
	Being courageous		
	Gaining knowledge		
	Feeling safe		

VALUES for Sale

# Available	Value	Worth to Me	Actual Cost

178

$25 $25 $50 $50 $100 $100

Everyday LEADERSHIP   Everyday LEADERSHIP   Everyday LEADERSHIP

$25 $25 $50 $50 $100 $100

$25 $25 $50 $50 $100 $100

Everyday LEADERSHIP   Everyday LEADERSHIP   Everyday LEADERSHIP

$25 $25 $50 $50 $100 $100

Making a
DIFFERENCE

After kids have built a leadership foundation and, ideally, have a greater understanding of their personal leadership potential, the sessions in this section will help teach them to make a difference by using all they've learned. The activities in this section emphasize broader discussions about taking risks, making the most of their personal leadership journeys, and taking steps to make an impact—for themselves and on others—in the present and for the future.

*Contains modifications for students transitioning to middle school

SESSION · SESSION · SESSION · SESSION
45

CHANGE THE
*World**

In this simple yet powerful activity, kids make posters that show how the world would look if they could change it. The activity inspires discussion about their community, the world around them, and how they feel they can make a difference. This is a good group-introduction activity; it is also useful as a preservice activity if kids are preparing to be involved in community service or advocacy efforts.

Time: 30–45 minutes (depending on group size and time allocated for presenting posters)

Age: Grades K–6

Group Size: No limit

LEADERSHIP LEARNING CONCEPTS

- Getting to Know Others
- Values
- Understanding Social Change

SUPPORTING STANDARDS

This activity supports content standards in ELA—Speaking and Listening, ELA—Writing, ELA—Language, Social Studies, and Service Learning (see pages 9–14 for details).

MATERIALS NEEDED

- markers, colored pencils, or crayons
- 9" x 12" or 12" x 18" construction or drawing paper

Contains modifications for students transitioning to middle school

Getting Ready

Place the paper, markers, pencils, and crayons in an area easily accessible to everyone in the group as they work on their posters.

Activity

Have kids select a piece of paper and several markers, pencils, or crayons. Then ask them to find a comfortable spot where they can think and draw on the paper. Before explaining the activity, select which one (or more, if you want kids to have a choice) of the following statements will be the prompt for your group.

- If I could change my school to make it a better place for everyone, this is what I'd do.

- If I could change my city to make it a better place for everyone, this is what I'd do.

- If I could change something in my life right now that will affect my future, this is what I'd change.

- If I could make the world a better place, this is what I'd do.

- If I could change the world, this is what I'd change and how the world would look after.

Explain to the group that each of them is going to create a poster that reflects their thoughts about a statement you will read to them. Their artistic ability doesn't matter. They simply need to think about the changes they would want if they had the power to make them happen, and create a poster with that in mind.

Read the statement or statements to your group and let them get started. Depending on the level of abstract or critical thinking skills of your group, you may need to provide suggestions or guidance. Do this by walking around the room offering suggestions and, if necessary, asking brief questions to help focus and clarify what each person may want to change. Encourage kids to use metaphors, quotes, poetry, symbols, drawings, colors, and other methods to express their perspectives. You may also give examples depending on the particular statement you pose. For example, you could say something like:

Maybe you want school to start at a different time and change how much time is spent on different subjects or activities. Maybe you'd like to see bullying go away. Maybe you'd like to see kids have more options and activities after school. Maybe you'd like to be able to travel or do a mission somewhere. Maybe you'd like to see a cure for a certain disease or the end of certain

social troubles; your changes might affect millions or they might make a smaller impact.

Once everyone has completed a poster, bring the group back together and have everyone take turns presenting their posters. Encourage kids to ask questions of one another, if appropriate. You may want to ask your own brief questions to further assist participants in expressing what they've drawn on their paper.

Talk About It

Using terms your students will understand, ask questions like the following to help explore the leadership learning:

- What was it like to think about changes you might make? What were the first images or ideas that came to mind?

- Do you feel like you can influence the future? Explain.

- Do you believe that one person can make a difference? Explain.

- How can you inspire people to help create the future described on your poster?

- What do you think you would hear if you asked this same question of others who are older or younger than you?

Middle School Transition Questions

If you are using this activity with fifth- and sixth-grade students who will be heading into middle school, consider including these questions during the discussion:

- How much thought do you give your future?

- How do you think the world will change between now and when you graduate from high school? Give specific examples.

- What are some goals you'd like to set for yourself? What can you do to give yourself the best chance to achieve them?

- What do you do when you're trying to make changes in your life, but it's hard? Examples might be trying to be more organized, trying to get higher grades, trying to find time to volunteer or join an after-school activity, or trying to help someone who is being bullied.

- Give an example of one thing you'd like to change in your life or in the world between today and the first day of middle school.

Middle School Transition Variation

If you're conducting this activity for middle school transition or to inspire kids to think about their future, you could use a prompt like this: "Think about your dream job. What does it look like? What would you be doing? As you work toward your career, what do you need to do to be prepared for your dream job? What changes do you need to make in your life to get ready?"

Variation

You may choose to revise or expand the prompt to address specific topics or core subject matter. For example, if the group is preparing to undertake a service project, you could phrase the question like this: "By the time your group finishes your service project, what impact do you hope to leave on the people you're serving? What kind of difference do you want to make for them?" Or for more global topics, you might phrase it: "If you were able to make a difference in the lives of people living in war or poverty, what would that difference look like? You can also show what it would look like if world leaders worked to make a long-lasting difference."

Extension

If space allows, hang the posters around the room or in a more visible hallway so others can look at, read, and think about them. Or, have kids create a bulletin board outside the room that poses the same question they answered, with blank paper and markers for others to write their responses.

CHOOSING
Sides*

Kids choose a side of the room to stand on to indicate whether they agree or disagree with each statement from a series of statements you read. They can also choose to stand on a line in the middle of the room, showing that they aren't sure or that their answer depends on the situation. Participants are also asked to explain why they have made their particular choice. This activity lends itself to rich discussions about respecting and understanding different viewpoints. You can use the statements provided, modify them, or write your own.

Time: 25–45 minutes (depending on group size and age)

Age: Grades K–6

Group Size: No limit

Note: For more mature groups or kids living in a community where complex social issues and prejudices may directly affect their lives daily, you may want to use the "Choosing Sides" statements on page 131 in *Teambuilding with Teens* by Mariam G. MacGregor, M.S. (Free Spirit Publishing, 2008). That list consists of statements that explore social issues, stereotypes, morality, and prejudices, and lead to discussions that benefit from higher-level thinking or firsthand experience.

LEADERSHIP LEARNING CONCEPTS

- Self-Awareness
- Tolerance and Diversity
- Understanding Social Change
- Values

SUPPORTING STANDARDS

This activity supports content standards in ELA—Speaking and Listening, Social Studies, and Service Learning (see pages 9–14 for details).

MATERIALS NEEDED

- masking tape
- 2 sheets of 8½" x 11" paper
- marker
- "Statements for Choosing Sides" handout (page 186 for grades 3–6 or page 187 for grades K–2)

Contains modifications for students transitioning to middle school

Getting Ready

Print a copy of the appropriate "Statements for Choosing Sides" handout and read it. Choose the statements that work best for your group and time limit. You may want to modify the list, add to it, or create your own list in order to appropriately challenge the kids in your group to think about new topics and stretch their thinking. Over time, you can compile statements from different groups you work with to add to your collection.

Move any tables, chairs, or desks out of the way to create an open area for movement. Lay a piece of masking tape across the middle of the floor to divide the room into two sides. Write "Agree" and "Yes" on one sheet of paper, and "Disagree" and "No" on another. Tape the sheets on opposite walls.

Activity

To start the activity, talk briefly about the difference between "fact" and "opinion." Sample explanation:

A fact is something that actually exists and is known to be true based on observation, research, or actual experience.

An opinion is a personal belief or view that may or may not be shared by others, and may not be true in all situations.

Ask kids to gather on one side of the room. Then explain:

The room has been divided into two sides. I am going to read a series of statements. If you agree with a statement or would answer yes to it, move to this side. (Gesture to the "yes" side.) **If you disagree or would answer no, move to the other.** (Gesture to the "no" side.) **The line of tape down the middle of the floor represents a choice of "I don't know" or "It depends on the situation." How you feel about some statements may be very clear to you. With others, you may struggle to decide where to stand. If you really can't choose, go to the middle, but only as a last resort. Either way, move to a spot that shows your opinion about the statement.**

After I've read a statement and everyone has moved, you can volunteer to explain why you're standing where you are. When others are talking, please listen and avoid judging, arguing, or trying to convince others to see things your way. Try to be open-minded and respectful about different points of view. Any questions?

Briefly answer any questions, and then begin. One by one, read the statements, allowing time for kids to move to their chosen spots and asking for volunteers to explain why they made the choice they did. Read as many statements as appropriate based on the time you have and how kids are responding.

If necessary, remind kids that when they're asked to share an opinion, it's just that—an opinion—and that all opinions are equally valuable and worthy of respect. Seeing how and where people move with each statement reminds the group that people can share some beliefs, yet not others, and that they may express them similarly or differently. There may be some surprises when kids move to a side that others aren't expecting.

When you have finished the selected statements, have kids sit where they landed last and discuss.

Talk About It

You may want to have kids point out the statements where most of the group shared the same values (everyone stood in one area), then, using terms your students will understand, ask questions like the following to help explore the leadership learning:

- What was your favorite statement? Why?

- What are some real-life situations where your friends or family expect you to act a certain way or believe a certain thing even though you don't? Explain. Did any of these confusing feelings or thoughts arise during this activity?

- Have you ever been in a situation where you were unable to let your true feelings show? What did you do? If you've never experienced this, what would you do if it happened?

- How can people be respectful of differing views or ideas? What if members of your group don't care what others think and want their views to drive the group's behavior?

- Were there any statements in this activity that you hadn't thought about before? If so, how did you decide how you felt about them? If you don't know what you believe about something in real life, how can you become aware and make a sound decision?

- Do you think it's important for leaders to have opinions about issues that affect the group? Why or why not?

- Are there any statements you would take off the list? Why? Any you would add?

Middle School Transition Questions

If you are using this activity with fifth- or sixth-grade students who will be heading into middle school, consider including these questions during the discussion:

- What will you do when you are new to middle school and disagree with what someone has said in the hallway or in a classroom? How will you speak up and make your own opinion known?

- Who can you turn to if you find yourself being judged or put-down for your views?

Variation

This is an excellent way to promote critical thinking for students in fifth or sixth grade, or when using this activity for middle school transition efforts. Rather than select from the list of statements included, ask each child (or small groups) to write down a statement related to real-life issues or concerns with which they think other kids agree or disagree. Provide an example or two from the list for guidance. Prior to conducting the activity, collect the statements. Set up the room and conduct the activity in the same way.

If you conduct the Variation, you may want to add a question or two such as:

- How easy or difficult was it to come up with a statement related to real-life issues or concerns?

- Were there any statements you wanted to submit but didn't? What kept you from turning in these statements? (For example, did you think others wouldn't understand or would judge you?)

- Do you feel there are any topics that people in your life (such as your family, friends, youth group, grandparents, faith organization) consider off-limits to talk, think, or worry about? If so, what are they? Why do you feel these topics are treated as off-limits?

Enrichments

1. Conduct the More Like Me activity (page 162) or the Would You Rather? activity (page 136) to delve deeper into personal values.

2. Divide kids into small work groups. Have each group create posters that vividly and succinctly state their views about one of the statements on the list of questions. Encourage teams to do research and include different opinions, stereotypes, or experiences people have about the statements. Display the posters where others can see them to inspire thinking and talking.

Statements for Choosing Sides (GRADES 3-6)

- It's okay to send someone a thank-you note by email instead of regular mail.

- It's okay for restaurants to ban kids who are younger than five from eating there.

- By the time I'm old enough to vote, a woman will be voted president of my country.

- The choices you make about your education, your friends, or your after-school activities when you are in elementary and middle school aren't important once you reach high school.

- Kids should be older than 12 to get a cell phone.

- If a homeless person approached me and asked for money, I would give the person some money.

- If I found $1,000 on a street in my neighborhood, with no name or information on it, I would turn it in to the police.

- Rich celebrities and professional athletes should be required to give a lot of their money to charity.

- I have bullied others.

- Girls are treated better at school by teachers than boys.

- Becoming famous is a goal of mine.

- Boys are more capable of becoming professional athletes than girls.

- Religion should be taught in school.

- A cure for most cancers will be discovered in my lifetime.

- If I had a chance to see the future, I would do it.

- Dogs are better than cats.

- Getting an allowance should be based on how much you help around your house.

- By the time I'm in college, laptop computers will be replaced by a different kind of technology.

- Racism (thinking one race is better than another) will always exist.

- I know what to do when I am being bullied or I see someone being bullied.

- I agree with everything my parents say.

- I believe the world will be a better place 100 years from now.

- There will always be a war happening somewhere in my lifetime.

- Kids know more about life than adults think they do.

- Being rich means you will be happy.

- Competition is a fact of life and makes everyone try their hardest.

- My parents let me make my own decisions.

- Learning how to speak more than one language should be required for every kid in our country.

- Students should be involved in hiring teachers for their school.

Statements for Choosing Sides (GRADES K-2)

- When playing sports against another team, no one should keep score.
- A cure for most cancers will be discovered during my lifetime.
- It's okay for restaurants not to allow kids younger than five to eat there.
- Learning how to speak more than one language should be required for every kid in our country.
- Dogs are better than cats.
- I know what to do when I am being bullied or I see someone being bullied.
- Kids know more about life than adults think they do.
- Being rich means you will be happy.
- Competition makes everyone try their hardest.
- If you don't learn how to use a computer, you will not be successful.
- Kids should be older than 12 to get a cell phone.
- I can make a positive difference in other people's lives.
- If I found $1,000 on a street in my neighborhood, with no name or information on it, I would turn it in to the police.

ZAPPING
Maze*

In this activity, kids attempt to solve a group task that can't be done unless people take risks and try new things. The risk involves figuring out which squares everyone needs to step on to get from one side of the maze to the other without getting "electrified" or "zapped."

Time: 45–60 minutes

Age: Grades 3–6

Group Size: 8–15 is best to maintain group engagement. Divide larger groups into smaller groups of 8–15 and have a maze for each group; additional facilitators are needed for each maze, because you will have all groups attempt the maze simultaneously.

Note: If your group has fifth and sixth graders preparing to enter middle school, consider using the teen version of this activity on page 113 of *Building Everyday Leadership in All Teens* by Mariam G. MacGregor, M.S. (Free Spirit Publishing, 2007). The differences include various penalties, a larger maze, a limited time period to finish the maze, and an emphasis in discussion on more complex risk taking related to being a teen leader.

LEADERSHIP LEARNING CONCEPTS

- Risk Taking
- Teamwork
- Problem Solving

SUPPORTING STANDARDS

This activity supports content standards in Math, Social Studies, and Service Learning (see pages 9–14 for details).

MATERIALS NEEDED

- 5' x 5' canvas painter's tarp (widely available at painter supply and do-it-yourself stores)
- masking tape
- "Zapping Maze Key" handout (page 192) or your own maze pattern using the "Blank Zapping Maze Key" (page 193)
- space to move around
- Optional: buzzer or other noise maker to indicate incorrect moves
- Optional: timer or clock

Contains modifications for students transitioning to middle school

Getting Ready

If you cannot find a 5' x 5' precut tarp, purchase a 10' x 20' plastic painter's tarp and fold it until you've reached the 5' x 5' dimension, then cut it to the correct size so that when kids are on the maze, it doesn't slip around.

Lay out the painter's tarp. Using masking tape, create a 5 x 5 grid of one-foot squares on the tarp by taping four lines horizontally one foot apart, and then crossing these with four taped lines going vertically on the tarp. (See "Zapping Maze Key" on page 192 for design.)

Place the completed maze in a location on the floor that allows space for kids to stand in groups and move around it. Tape the corners to the floor to prevent the maze from slipping or moving when individuals are standing upon it.

Make a copy of the "Zapping Maze Key," or design your own using the blank key. Use a folder or some other method to prevent kids from seeing this key at any time during the activity.

Activity

Begin this lesson with a discussion about taking risks. Ask students what it means to them to take a risk. What's the difference between taking dangerous risks and taking appropriate risks? To help them understand the difference, provide examples of dangerous risks and appropriate risks.

Dangerous risks

- not wearing a helmet when downhill skiing or riding bikes, dirt bikes, or motorcycles
- playing sports without the right equipment
- not wearing a seat belt
- running with scissors
- swimming in the dark or diving into a shallow pool

Appropriate risks

- running for student council, even if you have no experience
- trying out for your school play
- trying out for a new sport, even if you have no experience
- sitting next to new people during lunch
- speaking up or presenting new ideas to your team or group of friends

Next, talk more about appropriate risks by saying something like:

You may not even realize times when you take risks, such as when you work with others on school projects, plan and participate in service projects or youth group activities, or choose to take on positions that put you in the spotlight (such as school plays, student council, and solo performances).

Think of some appropriate risks you have taken in your life. Why did you take them? Think about what appropriate risks you might want to take in the future. Why might you take them?

Finally, what do we learn from taking appropriate risks? Does everyone learn the same thing or could everyone's experience, even if they're following the same path, be different because of the choices they make?

With your copy of the "Zapping Maze Key" in hand, ask kids to gather at the starting edge of the maze to begin the activity. To explain what everyone is to do, say:

With this discussion in mind, you're going to do an activity that focuses on taking risks and learning from those risks. Imagine the maze in front of you is "electrified" or "zapped," and there is only one correct path to get from where you're standing to the other end. Your goal as a team is to figure out what that path is without getting "zapped." From every square you can move sideways, forward, backward, or diagonally. Each step of the path is connected to the next. To get through, here are the team rules you'll follow:

- Only one person goes through the maze at a time.

- You have as much time as necessary to get through the maze, and everyone will follow the same path.

- Use as much time as you want to strategize, but once the first person steps on the maze, whether purposely or accidentally, you can no longer talk with one another. If anyone speaks after the first person has stepped on the maze, the person on the maze has to step off and begin again.

- If you step into the wrong box on the maze, I will "zap" you, which means you will have to retrace your steps to that point, step off the maze, and allow the next person to try.

- You may not leave any clues to your path on the maze or write them down. To guide whoever's on the maze, you may point to particular squares, but you may not touch the maze or say anything. If you do, you'll also get "zapped" and the person has to end their turn, retrace their path, and step off the maze.

Early on, everyone's turn is trial and error, since you don't know which squares are electrified. After your team figures out the path, each team member must follow it from start to finish until everyone has made it through successfully.

Any questions?

Allow time for questions, watching for people possibly touching the maze. If someone steps on it (deliberately or by accident), the activity begins and talking is no longer allowed.

Stand on the chair or stool, if you prefer, so you can clearly see kids as they move through the maze. Also pay attention to what others around the maze are doing. Initially, kids will stay at the starting end to watch whoever is on the maze, but as they get further through the maze, they will move around the edges and to the other end as they guide each other.

Each time someone takes a wrong step, use your voice or whatever noisemaker you chose to signify getting "zapped." Just as you beep, some participants may insist they were just "testing" a box (it wasn't a full step) or look at you but say nothing. During the Talk About It discussion, you may want to bring up this "testing." Talk about integrity, following rules, and respecting limitations even when taking risks.

It may be helpful to mark on your key the wrong squares kids repeatedly step on. During discussion, you may want to show kids how often they took the same path, even though it was wrong, and discuss how risk taking is about trying *new* paths instead of doing the same thing with unsuccessful results.

If everyone makes it through the maze, congratulate the group. If the group doesn't figure out the correct path, acknowledge their positive efforts and willingness to take a risk, and show them the answer. You can ask why the group wasn't successful during group discussion, encouraging them to figure out what, if anything, they could have done differently.

Talk About It

Before asking the following questions to explore leadership learning, offer your observations about how the group worked together. Point out the squares they incorrectly stepped on repeatedly, and ask them why they think they did. Using terms your students will understand, ask questions like the following to help explore the leadership learning:

- How did your group use its planning time? Do you think you used that time well? Why or why not? At what point did you realize that no matter how long you talked about getting through the maze, the thing your team most needed was to "just do it"?

- Are there any ways you think you could have worked more effectively as a team?

- Did the maze look different when you stood in the middle of it compared to when you stood outside of it? If so, why do you think that is? How can you relate this to your real life—and the idea of taking a risk (or trying something new) and then actually doing it?

- In life, how comfortable are you being the first one to do or try something new? Do you wish your comfort level was different? Explain.

- How do you think the group worked together? Where and how did you get stuck?

- Did anyone take on leadership roles? How did this help the team?

- In real life, how do you encourage others on your team or your friends to take risks or try new things?

- How can you learn from failures and successes when trying new things?

- Are you more or less motivated to take risks when you know others are watching? Explain.

- Is it important to maintain integrity (being honest, high standards) when taking risks? Why or why not?

- If relating this activity to social studies, ask: How is history affected by the risks or choices taken by different leaders?

- Can the path of history be changed by individuals or leaders, or does history repeat itself regardless of the choices and risks taken by leaders?

- If relating this activity to math, ask: What steps did you take to determine a pattern to the path?

- When you realized there was no pattern, how did you approach the task of solving the problem facing your group?

Middle School Transition Questions

If you are using this activity with fifth- or sixth-grade students who will be heading into middle school, consider including these questions during the discussion:

- What will you do when you find yourself in the middle of a problem thinking you're all alone? (Examples include having a difficult time understanding class material; being bullied or mocked during passing periods; being a new kid in town or at your school; having family problems; liking activities that others might consider childish; having family responsibilities or rules that make you feel like an outcast or like you're the only one with those expectations.)

- Who can you call on to help you make good choices and follow a path that makes you happy?

- When you've made choices that are troubling, what steps can you take to change your situation and try a new direction? What will you do when this choice is extremely difficult? (Examples: you start hanging around with new friends only to realize they're troublemakers or exclusionary to others; you want to forgo competitive sports but feel pressure from your parents or teammates to continue; you have difficulty with schoolwork and start slacking because you're not sure where to turn for help.)

Zapping Maze Key

The blackened boxes and step numbers show the correct path from the start to the end of the maze.

	10	9		
			8	7
		4		6
2	3		5	
1				

Zapping Maze Key

Create your own maze key by filling in step numbers in the grid.

SESSION · SESSION · SESSION · SESSION

48

IT COULD
Be Worse

This is an entertaining activity that promotes creative thinking and leadership aptitude by having kids react to an initial prompt, determine what can go wrong in that situation, and identify ways to make the situation better (or solve the problems that arise). This is a good icebreaker and group warm-up, especially if working with kids who have leadership responsibilities (such as student council, friendship group, or peer leadership) and expectations that they "fix" problems encountered by their group.

Time: 10–15 minutes (depending on group size)

Age: Grades 3–6

Group Size: No limit, although to ensure full engagement, you'll want to divide a large group into smaller groups of 5–8

LEADERSHIP LEARNING CONCEPTS

- Creative Thinking
- Understanding Social Change

SUPPORTING STANDARDS

This activity supports content standards in ELA—Speaking and Listening, Social Studies, and Service Learning (see pages 9–14 for details).

Getting Ready

Set up the room space in a manner that allows the group to sit in a circle. If the group is large, divide kids into smaller groups that will proceed through the activity simultaneously in independent circles.

Activity

Ask the group (or each group) to pick a person who will start the activity. They can get a volunteer or vote for someone. Then, explain that the first person will start by making a statement that describes the start of his or her day. The first half of the activity has things getting worse from that first example, but the second half of the activity has the group making things get better, therefore the initial statement should be neutral (or *nearly* bad), which allows things to go either way from what is said. Examples of first statements:

I almost overslept.

We were out of milk for breakfast.

I almost missed the bus.

The dog chewed the corner of my notebook.

Instruct the next player to start her or his response, which should relate to the first statement, by saying, "It could've been worse. You could have . . ." and say something that could have happened that would have been worse. For example:

. . . been late.

. . . been out of cereal.

. . . slipped on the ice.

. . . forgotten to do your homework.

Instruct the third player to say, "It could've been even worse than that, you could have . . ." Then the player should repeat what the second player said and add something even worse. For example, "It could've been even worse than that, you could have been late and you could've been in your underwear."

Everyone who follows repeats the phrase "It could've been even worse than that, you could have," repeats everything that has been said so far, and adds something worse to the end of the list. When the group has gone around once, the first person says, "It could have been better . . ." and starts a new list by saying a positive outcome. The next person says, "It could have been even better than that," repeats the previous outcome, and adds an even more positive outcome. Each subsequent person repeats the process until the group makes it around the circle again.

Talk About It

Encouraging kids to consider how some situations can go awry allows the freedom to explore how capable they are to turn around any sort of circumstance. Using terms your students will understand, ask questions like the following to help explore the leadership learning:

- What do you do when things aren't going your way?
- Who can you turn to for help when things go wrong?
- Do you get nervous in new situations or when you don't know what to expect? Explain.
- What can you do to find the sunny side of any situation?
- When you're the leader of a group and make a certain decision, what do you do when others expected a different decision, or they expected things to go a different way?

Variation

Use this activity to focus the group on a specific issue (such as a historical or political situation) or project (such as a service project they are about to start) that could be "worse" and how they can make it "better." Examples of first statements for this approach include:

The student council candy sale didn't raise much money.

Mrs. Varsa gave us too much homework.

We were expecting a sunny day for field day.

Not enough people tried out for the school play.

SUPPLIES NEEDED

Collect these items in a box (or the 5 gallon tub listed) and place in an easily accessible spot so you have a ready-to-use supply kit to conduct the sessions in this book. Review each session prior to conducting the activities to determine the specific items needed, as well as any perishable items that may be required.

General Supplies

- banner paper
- business-sized envelopes
- card stock (or other stiff paper) (8½" x 11")
- chart paper or dry-erase board and writing utensils
- colored pencils
- construction paper (8½" x 11")
- crayons
- index cards
- large manila envelopes (9" x 12")
- markers (wide and fine-point)
- masking tape
- newsprint
- pens/pencils
- plain white paper (8½" x 11")
- scissors
- stopwatch or digital watch with timer
- yarn and sturdy twine (thicker than yarn)

Unique and Optional Items

- adhesive name tags ("My Name Is")
- balloons (various sizes)
- bed sheet or blanket
- blindfolds or bandanas
- bouncy balls
- candy (individually wrapped)
- coin or other flat object with two unique sides
- dictionaries
- empty paper towel tubes
- golf balls
- hole punch
- jelly beans or other small candies, paper clips, small rubber erasers, etc.
- joke book (age-appropriate)
- large plastic berry container (empty and clean); see Time Capsule Transfer on page 147
- large plastic garbage bags
- Legos, Mega Bloks, or similar stick-together building blocks (such as math manipulatives)
- marbles
- medium-sized two-piece plastic eggs
- ping pong balls
- plastic painters' tarp or canvas painters' tarp (5' x 5' minimum)
- playground and/or other obstacles (hula hoops, chairs, stools, mats, milk crates, tunnels, etc.)
- pretend paper money, plastic coins, or bingo/poker chips
- PVC pipe tubes (2" diameter PVC cut into 12" lengths); see Pipeline on page 128
- raw eggs
- resealable plastic bags (sandwich or quart-sized)
- small pretzels (traditional shape or circles)
- interactive whiteboard
- soft balls and items of some weight (softball size or smaller, such as tennis or racquetball balls, small Nerf balls, stuffed animals, or bean bags)
- stamps
- straws
- tubs (2 gallon, or small, sturdy shoebox, and 5 gallon)
- unbroken spaghetti noodles in a box
- wooden platform or cinder blocks/paving stones; see Island Statues on page 131

Page references in **bold** refer to reproducible forms.

ABOUT THE AUTHOR

Mariam G. MacGregor, M.S., worked with student leaders at Syracuse University, Santa Clara University, and Metropolitan State College of Denver, before turning her energy to secondary education, integrating best-learned practices and innovative approaches to leadership development with kids and teens.

Mariam served as school counselor/coordinator of leadership programs at Vantage Point Alternative High School, where she worked with at-risk students, most of whom had never been involved in leadership experiences. She received Honorable Mention as Counselor of the Year for Colorado in 1999.

Mariam is now a nationally recognized leadership consultant who conducts leadership-specific staff development trainings, consults with schools and communities, and presents workshops emphasizing meaningful, sustainable, integrated leadership efforts. She contributes articles on leadership for various publications and published the widely used program development guidebook *Designing Student Leadership Programs: Transforming the Leadership Potential of Youth.* She was a contributing author to the leadership-based Girl Scouts of the USA Cadette curriculum, *aMaze,* which launched in 2008.

Her other books from Free Spirit include the award-winning *Building Everyday Leadership in All Teens: Promoting Attitudes and Actions for Respect and Success* and the companion teen guide *Everyday Leadership,* the activity guide *Teambuilding with Teens,* and *Everyday Leadership Cards: Writing and Discussion Prompts.* She lives in Texas with her husband and their three children. Contact Mariam at **www.mariammacgregor.com.**

Other Great Resources from Free Spirit

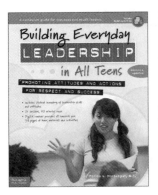

Building Everyday Leadership in All Teens
Promoting Attitudes and Actions for Respect and Success
by Mariam G. MacGregor, M.S.
Grades 6–12. 240 pp.;
paperback; 8½" x 11"
Includes digital content.

Requires the use of the student book, *Everyday Leadership.*

Teambuilding with Teens
Activities for Leadership, Decision Making, and Group Success
by Mariam G. MacGregor, M.S.
Grades 6–12.
192 pp.; paperback;
8½" x 11"
Includes digital content.

Everyday Leadership
Attitudes and Actions for Respect and Success
(A guidebook for teens)
by Mariam G. MacGregor, M.S.
Ages 11 & up. 144 pp.;
paperback; 7" x 9"

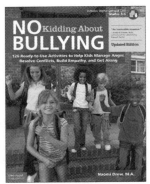

No Kidding About Bullying
126 Ready-to-Use Activities to Help Kids Manage Anger, Resolve Conflicts, Build Empathy, and Get Along (Updated Edition)
by Naomi Drew, M.A.
Grades 3–6. 304 pp.;
paperback; 8½" x 11"
Includes digital content.

Everyday Leadership Cards
Writing and Discussion Prompts
by Mariam G. MacGregor, M.S.
Ages 10 & up. 60 cards; 2-color;
3" x 4½"

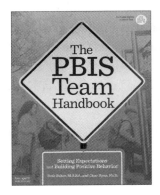

The PBIS Team Handbook
Setting Expectations and Building Positive Behavior
by Beth Baker, M.S.Ed., and Char Ryan, Ph.D.
Grades K–12.
208 pp.; paperback;
8½" x 11"
Includes digital content.

Interested in purchasing multiple quantities and receiving volume discounts?
Contact edsales@freespirit.com or call 1.800.735.7323 and ask for Education Sales.

Many Free Spirit authors are available for speaking engagements, workshops, and keynotes.
Contact speakers@freespirit.com or call 1.800.735.7323.

For pricing information, to place an order, or to request a free catalog, contact:

Free Spirit Publishing Inc. • 6325 Sandburg Road • Suite 100 • Minneapolis, MN 55427-3674
toll-free 800.735.7323 • local 612.338.2068 • fax 612.337.5050
help4kids@freespirit.com • www.freespirit.com